Recantation and Domestic Violence

Recantation and Domestic Violence empowers people and communities in improving their understanding of and skills in domestic violence cases that involve recantation. This book illustrates the precise interpersonal dynamics of recantation in criminal cases in which felony-level abuse has occurred.

This book equips professionals in working more effectively with victims of domestic violence, their abusers, family members, and other supporters. Using the *five-stage model* of recantation, case examples, and audiotaped telephone conversations between abusers and their victims, it puts the reader directly in touch with what abusers say, how they say it, and how victims respond.

This book is applicable to practitioners and research audiences in fields such as criminal law, family law, child custody, violence prevention, therapeutic interventions, medicine, nursing, psychology, social work, sociology, and behavioral economics.

Amy Bonomi, PhD, MPH, is Professor and Associate Dean of Strategic Initiatives in the College of Health and Human Services at Northern Arizona University, Founder of Social Justice Associates, Faculty Affiliate at the Harborview Injury Prevention and Research Center, and Consultant for the U.S. Department of Justice. Bonomi's distinguished career as an award-winning professor at the Ohio State University and Michigan State University includes widely cited research on domestic violence, recantation, and long-term health impacts. Bonomi and her research team (including David Martin) published the *five-stage model* of how domestic abusers tamper with and coerce victims to recant. The *five-stage model* (along with the team's subsequent publications) has been used to train professionals globally. Bonomi continues the practice of expert testimony work to describe the dynamics of recantation. As a result of her work in recantation and broader domestic violence topics, Bonomi received the Distinguished Scholar Award from the Ohio State University and was named Diversity Champion in the College of Social Science at Michigan State University. Bonomi is appointed by the U.S. Health and Human Services Secretary (Xavier Becerra) as Chair of the Board of Scientific Counselors for the National Center for Injury Prevention and Control and serves as an elected peer reviewer (for violence prevention research) for the U.S. Centers for Disease Control and Prevention and the National Institute of Justice.

David Martin, JD, is Senior Deputy Prosecutor for the King County Prosecuting Attorney's Office (KCPAO) in Seattle, Washington. He serves as Supervisor of the KCPAO Domestic Violence (DV) unit, Comanager of the King County Regional DV Firearms Enforcement Unit, and Fulbright Specialist in Domestic Violence Response. Almost all of his 25-year career as a prosecutor has been spent in the DV unit. Martin has created innovative responses to serve victims of DV from the first evidence rule on immigration to systemic provision of civil legal aid in criminal cases, to diversion and sentence alternatives for defendants with past histories of gender violence victimization. Martin serves on numerous DV task forces and work groups, is Co-Chair of the national Association of Prosecuting Attorney's DV Committee. He has authored several of Washington's criminal DV laws including felony sentencing reform, removal of the marital rape exception, stalking reform, batterer treatment reform, felony strangulation, and repeat DV assault. Martin is coauthor of Washington's statewide DV prosecution manual, articles on strangulation, and recantation together with Dr. Amy Bonomi. He has served on the board of multiple community-based DV organizations. He provides training and consultation on DV issues locally, nationally, and internationally. He is the recipient of the Prosecuting Attorney's Outstanding Trial Advocacy Award, Lifewire Norm Maleng Award, Consejo Founder's Award, and Coalition Ending Gender Based Violence System Change Award.

Recantation and Domestic Violence

The Untold Story

Amy Bonomi and David Martin

Routledge
Taylor & Francis Group
LONDON AND NEW YORK

Designed cover image: gettyimages.com/Antonio M. Rosario

First published 2024
by Routledge
4 Park Square, Milton Park, Abingdon, Oxon OX14 4RN

and by Routledge
605 Third Avenue, New York, NY 10158

Routledge is an imprint of the Taylor & Francis Group, an informa business

British Library Cataloguing-in-Publication Data
A catalogue record for this book is available from the British Library

Library of Congress Cataloging-in-Publication Data
Names: Bonomi, Amy, author. | Martin, David, author.
Title: Recantation and domestic violence : the untold story / Amy Bonomi, David Martin.
Description: Abingdon, Oxon [UK] ; New York : Routledge, 2023. | Includes bibliographical references and index. | Contents: Recantation : direct byproduct of abuser tampering—Five-stage model : what abusers say, how they say it, how victims respond—Recapping the five-stage model-its limitations and strengths—So this is where you think I need to be? (Case Example 1)—If I lost you, it's like losing an arm or something (Case Example 2)—She needs to show up tomorrow and say she was lying (Case Example 3)—Feed and nurture the "good wolf" (Case Example 4)—Your mom is mean and evil (Case Example 5)—The five-stage model, jail calls : relationship to coercive control, family systems, and attachment theories—Using the five-stage model and jail calls to advance community response to domestic violence.
Identifiers: LCCN 2023027520 (print) | LCCN 2023027521 (ebook) | ISBN 9781032391687 (hardback) | ISBN 9781032391670 (paperback) | ISBN 9781003348696 (ebook) | ISBN 9781032606217 (ebook other)
Subjects: LCSH: Family violence—Law and legislation. | Marital violence—Law and legislation. | Wife abuse—Law and legislation. | Abused wives—Legal status, laws, etc. | Women—Crimes against—Law and legislation. | Victims of crimes—Legal status, laws, etc.
Classification: LCC K5190 .B66 2023 (print) | LCC K5190 (ebook) | DDC 362.82/92—dc23/eng/20231002
LC record available at https://lccn.loc.gov/2023027520
LC ebook record available at https://lccn.loc.gov/2023027521

ISBN: 978-1-032-39168-7 (hbk)
ISBN: 978-1-032-39167-0 (pbk)
ISBN: 978-1-003-34869-6 (ebk)
ISBN: 978-1-032-60621-7 (eBook+)

DOI: 10.4324/9781003348696

Typeset in Sabon
by Apex CoVantage, LLC

Contents

Preface

David Martin

I grew up in a home with domestic violence, where my father abused my mother. It was the 1980s, so when police came to our house for domestic violence, they would just tell us to "keep it down." In high school, I intervened and fought with my father. It was a fight I lost badly. That was the last time I saw my father.

Because of my childhood experience, I know what happens behind closed doors and decided to dedicate my life to trying to end domestic violence. I became a criminal prosecutor. I have spent the last 25 years prosecuting domestic violence cases and developing practices and policies that aim to help victims and hold abusers accountable.

My professional home for the past 25 years is the King County Courthouse. It's in an old building. A building that is musty. A building that is too hot in the summer, too cold in the winter. The courtrooms and offices appear suspended in time, in a part of downtown Seattle that seems to have been bypassed by economic development and modern advancements.

In the spring of 2005, I was reviewing cases for upcoming jury trials. At that time, our domestic violence cases were in paper files. We reviewed police reports, victim statements, and a cassette tape or compact disc with a 911 recording. There were no body-worn police cameras, social media posts, or recordings of the victims or abusers. Victim recantation happened regularly. Victims and victim advocates wrote letters explaining why the victim did not want to participate in prosecution, denied the abuse happened, or blamed something or someone else. As prosecutors, we believed the abuser was responsible for the victim's recantation but rarely could prove it.

When an abuser was in custody, we would order phone call records from the jail. In our cases, courts often impose "no-contact" orders prohibiting the abuser from contacting the victim. We regularly requested phone records to determine whether someone at the jail called the victim's phone number or called to find out which cell block the abuser was held in. We also worked to determine if calls originated from those specific cell blocks, and we would then investigate whether the calls tracked when the abuser moved from cell block to cell block. This could show circumstantially that the abuser was contacting the victim. We never heard the calls, never listened to what was said, and never thought we would be able to.

One day in 2005, I reviewed a case where the victim recanted and had called the jail. I suspected there had been witness tampering, where the abuser had called the victim and coerced her to recant. Unbeknownst to us prosecutors, the jail had a new system that recorded inmate phone calls. The jail offered us recordings of the phone calls made from jail. Days later, I was listening to the recorded jail calls.

The content of those jail calls was painfully familiar. The abuser calling the victim sounded like my dad. The victim sounded like my mom. They argued about what had happened, i.e., how he had abused her. In call after call, the abuser pled with the victim to recant and relieve him from the charges. Nothing prepares a person to hear what abuse sounds like, even for those who have heard it before. For the first time, I listened to an abuser call a victim, and in the process, violate a court order restraining that contact, manipulate, tamper, and abuse the victim all over again. Listening was like reliving my childhood.

I shared the jail-call recordings with the abuser's attorney. He quickly offered to settle the case. The weeks and months that followed were a whirlwind. The jail calls rapidly became known as a method for bolstering convictions. However, the calls were contested. Were jail calls legal? Was it proper? Legal briefings, motions, and rulings soon came in our favor: recording jail calls was legal. Courts found that the abuser knew the calls would be recorded and had no reasonable expectation of privacy, and therefore, the recordings were admitted as evidence against the abuser. The decision to make jail calls legal was upheld in *State v. Modica*: 164 Wash.2d. 186 P. 3d 1062, Wash. July 10, 2008, and has been since further upheld in multiple additional cases (e.g., *State v. Archie*, 148 Wn. App. 198, 2009, and *State v. Donato*, 4 Wn. App. 2d 1081, 2018).

In the months and years that followed, we established the admissibility of jail calls as evidence in court. Yet, jail calls between abuser and victim represented something much more critical to domestic violence than their use only in prosecution. There was something essential to learn about domestic violence from jail calls. The calls were not just familiar to me because I grew up in a home with domestic violence, but they were critical to understanding the cycle of domestic violence. No one in the court system had heard what domestic violence sounded like before. Now there were hours and hours of recorded calls. Today, there are millions of hours.

I called the University of Washington to ask for advice on how to begin delving into the jail calls in a more systematic fashion to advance the field's understanding of domestic violence. I was referred to Prof. Amy Bonomi, a research affiliate at the University of Washington's Harborview Injury Prevention and Research Center. I was fortunate to meet Amy. I brought compact discs from cases and asked if Amy would listen to them to help understand what the calls revealed about domestic violence. She patiently answered my questions and was deeply impacted by the information.

Amy was recruited from Seattle to the Ohio State University and spent years on research with her teams of graduate and undergraduate students to examine the jail calls through the lens of public health and social science to craft a cohesive understanding of domestic violence. What followed was, for me, a fantastic opportunity to learn, follow, and partner with one of the leading experts on domestic violence. Amy was then and is today an incredibly gracious, brilliant, and thoughtful researcher, mentor, and colleague.

Amy's analysis of the jail calls is groundbreaking. She analyzed and distilled the recordings of phone calls between abusers and their victims to show an evidence-based, empirical cycle of manipulation and deceit by abusers. She showed how abusers pressured their victim to recant, not through threats and intimidation, but with strategies such as appealing to the victim's sympathy and conjuring images and memories of earlier, happier times together. The processes abusers used were effective. Abusers' manipulation of the victim was so successful in part because they were pressuring the victim to engage in normative behavior (to remain in the relationship and maintain the relationship) even though the relationship was characterized by significant harm.

Amy's work represents a paradigm shift in knowledge and understanding of domestic violence. Amy's work remains today the only research that focuses on jail calls—a significant source of empirical data to help us understand the second-by-second interactions that occur between abusers and victims to influence recantation. Amy's analysis of calls between abusers and victims must serve as an unparalleled resource that is incorporated into domestic violence education, policy, and future research.

Amy's *five-stage model* (described later) distilling the jail calls enables listeners to step into the room with kids like me to live the experience and listen to what goes on in a domestic violence relationship. Thanks to Amy's research, there is much more that our broader communities can learn and do. All it takes to start is to press play and listen.

Amy Bonomi

Our book is about human interactions—the second-to-second ebb and flow of emotions and behaviors. It is about how abusers tamper with those second-to-second interactions to influence their victim's intention to recant—to take back the story they told to police, the domestic violence advocate, the judge. It is also about the "everyday" nature of conversations—what gets said, how it gets said, and how people respond—in between tampering. From conversations about brushing teeth, sleep patterns, struggles at work, how pets are doing, how children are doing, getting the car in for repairs, to conversations about emotional connection and longing.

When David Martin first approached me in 2005 about the potential of using jail calls to explore what is known about domestic violence, I was both intrigued and eager to get started. Studying the jail calls with David Martin—a well-respected practitioner in the community and rising star in the national policy realm—was an unprecedented opportunity. I am a qualitative researcher, have always been drawn to human narratives, and studied, in my doctoral program with David Allen (Professor Emeritus, University of Washington), qualitative inquiry as it pertains to violence against women.

Despite my eagerness to start working on the jail calls, my schedule over the next two years permitted only a few meetings and phone conversations with David Martin. I was in the middle of a cross-country transition from the University of Washington and Kaiser Washington Research Institute to the Ohio State University to start my first academic position as an associate professor.

Roughly two years after settling into academia, I obtained approval from the Ohio State University's human subjects committee to begin studying the jail calls. Partnering with David Martin, I began listening to and rigorously analyzing the calls with a team of doctoral students including Rashmi Gangamma (the Ohio State University's Couple and Family Therapy Program and now associate professor at the University of Colorado Denver), Heather Katafiasz (the Ohio State University's Couple and Family Therapy Program and now associate professor at the University of Akron), and Christopher Locke (the Ohio State University's Social Work Program and now Major and Clinical Social Worker with the United States Army).

Given our collective professional backgrounds and familiarity with domestic violence theories focused on patriarchal control, when we began listening to the jail calls, our team anticipated (and confirmed) hearing abuser manipulation and tampering. However, our team was not fully prepared for what we heard. It was far more than what we had studied, read about, written about, and observed in clinical interactions and when running treatment groups with abusers. We were listening in on humanity uninterrupted—hearing every second-by-second change in emotions, speech, and silence. More often than silence, we heard pets and children in the background, music couples listened to, discussions about movies and books, sighs, crying, pauses, longing for each other, sexual cravings, and hopes and dreams.

And while abusers and victims knew their calls were being recorded, they communicated with each other as if no one was listening.

Our team heard abusers' manipulation—the kind of manipulation that David Martin and prosecutors use as evidence of tampering. And we heard hours and hours of "everyday" conversation. The undergraduate students who transcribed the jail-call audiotapes often commented that the "everyday" conversations sounded "exactly like" conversations with their own boyfriends. For example, an undergraduate student detailed lengthy conversations one couple had about the film *Aliens*. However, the "everyday" conversations we listened to were part of a larger pattern of manipulation following severe felony-level violence—the focus of the couples we studied. And as such, the "everyday" conversations could not be divested from the severe harm that had been inflicted upon victims with the threat of future violence constantly looming (even though not often threatened during the calls we listened to).

From our interactions with and rigorous analysis of the jail calls, our research team developed a *five-stage model* that delineates how abusers and victims interacted to influence recantation—a process manipulated by the abuser, yet a process that involved victims and abusers expressing their needs for emotional connection and intimacy. The *five-stage model*, supporting exemplars, and extensions of the model are the focus of our book.

Throughout the study of jail calls, David Martin has been, and continues to be, a brilliant and insightful practice partner, mentor, and coauthor. David helped us see how our research discoveries could be used in court, and how those discoveries could be used to advance practitioners' understanding of working with victims who recanted. David has always drawn our attention to the reality that while it is tempting for practitioners to take cases involving recantation less seriously, our *five-stage model* points to just the opposite: we need to redouble our efforts in cases involving recantation.

David and I have continued to develop ideas and write about the jail calls. Our subsequent publications together have examined how abusers triangulate third parties (children, friends, family members) to influence victim recantation, how different technology modalities (e.g., text messages) are now used by abusers to tamper with victims, and how victim advocates have successfully worked to interrupt abuser tampering through text messaging with victims. In addition, our research team studied the jail calls to examine acute and situational factors (within the ecological model) that drive violence in relationships—a publication led by Julianna Nemeth, former doctoral student and now assistant professor of Public Health at the Ohio State University.

Collectively, our book ties together our new ideas learned from jail calls with our original study, which resulted in the *five-stage model* presented in the book about what abusers say, how they say it, and how victims respond in the process of recantation. Our book illustrates the second-by-second interactions between abusers and victims within the broader context of being human.

As you delve into the jail calls included in our book, we offer a reminder that what you will hear reflects the experiences of real people, their lives, and their experiences of abuse. The jail calls are, at times, very difficult to listen to because listening involves being present with abuse. Our research team experienced secondary trauma listening to and analyzing the jail calls. Graduate students (in Couple and Family Therapy, Psychology, and Social Work programs) enrolled in my course *Violent Family Systems* at the Ohio State University described a "tower of anxiety" that they felt when listening to the jail calls—a direct impact of being present to abuse.

Readers of the print version of our book can access the jail recordings by visiting our website at: https://recantation.org/.

To protect the identity of the cases presented in the book, we have undertaken extraordinary precautions by altering names (in consultation with colleagues, we intentionally chose names that could reflect people from any number of cultural identities) and contextual details (such as geographic locations). And we have taken precaution to present the most balanced interpretation possible about what domestic violence sounds like "live" when listening to recordings. Still yet, we are open to your interpretations and hope you will be in touch with us to share your perspectives.

Our hope is that this book will encourage others to use existing empirical evidence to delve deeper into understanding the nature of domestic violence. There are no easy answers in attempting to understand or respond to domestic violence. Human beings and human relationships are complex. This book is a new path to address the historical and ongoing generational toll of abuse. We hope others join us on the path.

Foreword

One of the long-standing frustrations of those in the criminal justice system working with victims of intimate partner ("domestic") violence is when they file charges against the abuser and later recant. Victims almost never call the police unless the abuse has gotten really serious and they are afraid, and at first they want the abuser arrested and out of the home so that she and the children could be safe. Despite all our rhetoric about "holding abusers accountable," this is a criminal justice construct, not what I hear abused women say. I have interviewed more than 3,000 abused women myself—either personally in various studies or in talking to them about their experiences in the Danger Assessment (www.dangerassessment.org). I have heard many women talk about calling the police because they were terrified; I have seldom heard them say that they wanted their abuser to go to jail, except maybe for a few days to "cool off" and to give her a little space. Think what a complex decision that would be if you were to weigh the pros and cons of putting your partner in jail for more than a little while—the issues of him being unable to provide for your children, to help pay the mortgage or rent, and the probability that conviction and jail time will mean he will lose his job and may become unemployable. She will have to explain to their children and to his family why she did that to him and justify how scared and desperate she was. Many times, when I do a Danger Assessment with women and their score is at Severe or Extreme Danger (the most dangerous levels), they will feel empowered by knowing their fear was justified, that calling the police was a reasonable, smart, self- and child-preserving and protecting thing to do. It is almost impossible for those of us who have not been abused by a partner to understand the behavior of women who are experiencing violence. When we read *Recantation and Domestic Violence* that so brilliantly analyzes the jailhouse calls of abusers who are trying to get their partners to recant, to get them out of jail, perhaps we begin to understand how and why victims of domestic violence "behave" the way they do. Of course, it doesn't take great theoretical understanding of human behavior to comprehend how abusers operate through coercion and manipulation. But understanding the complexity of women's response can be far more difficult. As you read *Recantation and Domestic Violence*, Amy and David help to provide an understanding of both victim and abuser behavior in ways that are unprecedented. As you read and listen, try to understand the many deep and terrible ambivalences of the abusers' partners. The reality of once, even if not now, loving him deeply, the wonderful memories you have of him and your times together and how he can be wonderful and is often now, the practicalities of the situation and your and your children's future, the possibilities that people can change, the desperate wanting to believe that he will. Imagine how just hearing his voice brings back good memories, and then when you hear anger and threats in that voice, how it might "trigger" you, put you into a place of absolute terror and irrational thinking that makes you think you have to do what he says. And a terrible knowledge that if you don't recant, the sentence he serves will probably not be very long, that prison never made a person become less violent without some sort of treatment with it, and that you will need to take your children to visit him in prison unless you want them to feel resentment of you. Never underestimate the powerful motives of women experiencing violence trying to be good mothers in this almost impossible situation. *Recantation and Domestic Violence* is powerful, important, and timely. We need more research and composite case examples like this to help us understand the complexities of domestic violence and how we as a society can do better in our approach to this issue so that women and their children can stay safer. We need ways to identify and intervene when the abuse is in early stages, when abusers have access to interventions before it gets so bad that arrest and incarceration result, and the many pressures from society and from him and from the abused own psyche to recant don't have such power.

Jacquelyn Campbell, PhD, RN, FAAN
Professor
Anna D. Wolf Chair
School of Nursing
Johns Hopkins University

Acknowledgments

We are deeply grateful for the significant contributions and support we received from people, organizations, communities, and publishers that granted us permission to reprint our previously published work.

First, we acknowledge the significant contributions of our coauthors in the original jail-call paper resulting in the *five-stage model* published in *Social Science and Medicine*, Dr. Rashmi Gangamma (University of Colorado Denver), Dr. Christopher Locke (United States Army), and Dr. Heather Katafiasz (University of Akron). Dr. Gangamma was a main analyst in conceptualizing the *five-stage model* and for catalyzing our orientation to the interpersonal nature of the interactions between abusers and victims. Dr. Christopher Locke and Dr. Heather Katafiasz worked closely with Drs. Bonomi and Gangamma in the analysis of the jail calls and development of the *five-stage model.* Drs. Gangamma, Locke, and Katafiasz expanded our thinking that abuse is a "one-way process" of the abuser tampering with the victim to reimagine the interpersonal nature of interactions, the ebb and flow of emotions and behaviors. Dr. Gangamma continues to use the original jail-call study in her training of doctoral and master's students at the University of Colorado Denver. Dr. Locke has continued to present the jail-call work to clinical audiences throughout the United States in his role with the United States Army. Continuations of the *five-stage model* have been published in the *Journal of Family Violence*, and we are grateful to Dr. Rebecca Macy (Editor-in-Chief) for her support of the work.

Former graduate students (Dr. Julianna Nemeth, Dr. Christin Carotta, Dr. Megan Lee, Dr. Pooja Khariwal, Elizabeth Cannon, and Jennifer Ludwin) and undergraduate students (Lynsey Terrell, Julia Sweeney, Sara Schiavone, and Stephanie Blatnick) of the Ohio State University led additional important analyses, publications, and presentations pertaining to the jail calls. For example, Dr. Nemeth led an analysis of the jail calls using an events perspective and the ecological model to understand acute and chronic stressors that gave rise to the abuse event resulting in the abuser's detention. Former undergraduate students at the Ohio State University—Ashley Lomax, James Miller, Anthony Perez, and Stef (Dimofski) Ziegler—worked with Dr. Bonomi to reenact the jail calls for campus audiences to provide education on the dynamics of abuse. Former undergraduate students also of the Ohio State University—Melissa Padalino, Molly Van Hart, Elizabeth Farrar, Kaci Hathaway, Caitlin Havens, Amanda Lee, and Jessica Varga—assisted with transcribing the audiotapes. Dr. Debra Moddelmog, while at the Ohio State University, conducted thoughtful reviews of Dr. Bonomi's grant proposals that focused on analyzing the jail calls.

Sandra Shanahan (Director of the Regional Domestic Violence Firearms Enforcement Unit, and former director of the Protection Order Advocacy Program in the King County Prosecuting Attorney's Office) provided critical feedback to strengthen the relevance of the book for professional audiences.

Laura J. Young (graduate of the English and Communication programs of the University of Michigan and ordained United Methodist minister) provided critical editorial review and feedback to strengthen the clarity of the book for a range of audiences.

Evi Judge (graduate of the Linguistics program at the University of Colorado Boulder) assisted with preparing the audio-recordings for inclusion in the book.

Our beloved family and friends provided steady, ongoing support. Amy Bonomi especially acknowledges the love and support while writing the book foremost from Margaret ("Madge") Judge; Robin Deterding; Asia Eaton; Dionne Stephens; Pamela Malzbender; Dawn Weber; Philip, Linda, and Tom Bonomi; Jean Ruth; and her extended family. Amy is also grateful for research support pertaining to domestic violence from many colleagues, especially those from the University of Washington, the Harborview Injury Prevention and Research Center, and the Kaiser Washington Research Institute, including Frederick Rivara, Robert ("Tommy") Thompson, Melissa Anderson, Paul Fishman, David Allen, Victoria Holt, Diane Martin, and Sharyne Shiu-Thornton. David Martin especially acknowledges the love and support of his spouse Aurora Martin; his children, Hannah and Jonah; his mother, Julie Elliott; sisters, Claudia and Laura; and his extended family. David is also grateful for the support, guidance, and mentorship of his prosecutor, advocate, legal service professional, and community colleagues, both past and present. Their work of serving victims and seeking justice continues to inspire.

Last, we want to acknowledge and convey our deep gratitude to the many domestic violence victims—those we have interacted with, those we have lost, and those throughout the world with narratives we all must hear. Your profound narratives inspired and informed every word of the book. Our book is for you and for all victims whose narratives, experiences, strengths, vulnerabilities, despair, and hope contribute to a more inclusive understanding of how to help those impacted by domestic violence and society.

Organizations

We are grateful for funding provided to Dr. Bonomi to analyze the jail calls from the Criminal Justice Research Center of the Ohio State University (Columbus, Ohio) and the Group Health Foundation (Seattle, Washington).

We are thankful to the many deputy prosecutors, victim advocates, and legal service professionals in the King County Prosecuting Attorney's Office Domestic Violence Unit, the United States Department of Justice, and many other organizations whose work serving victims and seeking justice is reflected in this book. We thank the King County Department of Adult and Juvenile Detention for providing infrastructure support and access to the jail audio-recordings, to the Ohio State University for providing infrastructure, research and teaching support, along with support for communicating our work to broader audiences (specifically Jeff Grabmeier, Senior Director of Research Communications, and Joe Camoriano, Director of National Broadcast Media), and to the Harborview Injury Prevention and Research Center where Amy Bonomi is currently an affiliate faculty member and David Martin is a regular collaborator in violence prevention research.

We thank numerous organizations that have invited us to present our work and provided feedback for informing the *five-stage model* and subsequent work. These presentations included (and were led by) many members of our research team mentioned earlier:

- Advances in Qualitative Methods Conference
- American Association for Marriage and Family Therapy Conference
- American Psychological Association Annual Convention
- American Public Health Association Annual Meeting
- Association for Women in Psychology Annual Conference
- Association of Prosecuting Attorneys, Domestic Violence Committee
- Aid to Victims of Domestic Abuse Awareness Benefit
- Bar of Northern Ireland
- Coalition Ending Gender-Based Violence
- Columbus Coalition Against Family Violence
- Dialogue for Hope (Canton, Ohio)
- Domestic Violence Coordinating Council of Hamilton County (Cincinnati, Ohio)
- Domestic Violence Symposium, King County Prosecuting Attorney STOP Grant Managers
- Estonian Ministry of Justice
- European Conference on Domestic Violence (Norway, Slovenia, and Iceland)
- Family Violence Prevention Summit, Ohio Domestic Violence Network
- Front Range Community College
- Harborview Injury Prevention and Research Center
- Mesa County Intimate Partner Violence Awareness Conference
- Michigan Prosecuting Attorney Association Annual Meeting
- Michigan State University College of Human Medicine
- National Conference on Health and Domestic Violence
- National Council on Family Relations Conference
- National District Attorneys Association, Women Prosecutors Section
- Ohio Attorney General's Office Two Days in May Conference
- Ohio Department of Rehabilitation and Correction
- Ohio State University College of Medicine
- Ohio State University Sexuality Studies Program
- Ohio State University Women, Gender, and Sexuality Studies Program
- Qualitative Health Research Conference
- Republic of Georgia, Prosecution Service and Ministry of Justice
- Seattle University School of Law
- State of Idaho Council on Domestic Violence and Victim Assistance
- Supreme Court Advisory Board, State of Ohio
- Transitions, Inc. Annual Benefit (Zanesville, Ohio)
- University of Denver HerDU Conference
- University of Rochester
- University of Washington
- Washington Association of Prosecuting Attorneys
- Washington State Coalition Against Domestic Violence
- Women, Gender and Violence Conference, Florida International University
- Women's Health Congress
- Women's Health Summit
- Zonta Foothills of Boulder County

Reprinting Acknowledgments

Elsevier Publishers granted us permission to reprint (in original and in modified form) the following publication in our book:

- Bonomi, A.E., R. Gangamma, C.R. Locke, H. Katafiasz, and D. Martin. 2011. " 'Meet me at the hill where we used to park:' Interpersonal processes associated with victim recantation." *Social Science and Medicine* 73: 1054–1061.

Springer Nature granted us permission to reprint (in original and in modified form) the following publications:

- Bonomi, A.E., and D. Martin. 2018. "Jail calls: What do kids have to do with it." *Journal of Family Violence* 33 (2): 99–102.
- Bonomi, A.E., and D. Martin. 2020. "Domestic abusers: Expert triangulators, new victim advocacy models to buffer against it." *Journal of Family Violence* 36: 383–388.

The book contains disturbing images and accounts and retelling of domestic violence and abuse incidents. Reader discretion is advised.

1 Recantation
Direct By-product of Abuser Tampering

The Case of Shawn and Tasha

Tasha called 911—the emergency number for reaching the police and firefighters in the United States—scared for her life. Her boyfriend, Shawn, had just strangled her, and she momentarily lost consciousness. When police arrived, Tasha told them what happened, and Shawn was arrested. This was not the first time that Shawn had strangled Tasha. In fact, Shawn had strangled Tasha dozens of times in the prior 12 months.

When police left, Tasha was alone, and soon Shawn called her from jail. Shawn said he was sorry, he missed Tasha, and he loved her. Tasha did not forgive Shawn, but as she hung up the phone, her neck still sore, she was willing to talk to Shawn again.

Shawn continued to call from jail, dozens of times—17 hours' worth. Shawn pressured Tasha to recant—to take back what she'd told police. As Shawn pressured Tasha, he reminded her about what life would be like without each other, about how he wanted to marry her, and about how his depression was getting worse and he felt like killing himself. Shawn also reminded Tasha of how "fucked" (unfair) the criminal justice system is and how together as a couple they would overcome this "latest bump" and build an even stronger life together as "husband and wife." Shawn and Tasha were not married, yet Shawn regularly held out promises to marry Tasha and routinely characterized their roles as "husband and wife."

Shawn's phone calls to Tasha were recorded. Recording jail calls is now routine procedure in jails throughout the United States, a practice upheld in a Washington State Supreme Court decision (*State v. Modica*, 164 Wash.2d. 186 P. 3d 1062, Wash. July 10, 2008, NO. 79767–6).

Shawn's phone calls to friends were also recorded, whereby he instructed friends to threaten Tasha, hurt her, and rape her if she did not agree to retract her statement:

Shawn: You need to fucking talk to her tonight . . . tell her she needs to either not show up or she needs to show up tomorrow and say that she was lying. If she shows up tomorrow and says she was lying, I get out, feel me? . . . It's important that I talk to her. Can you hear me?

Friend: Yeah. You want me to pass her that number or what do you want me tell her?

Shawn: I want you to show up to her fucking work, man . . . give her that fucking number and tell her to fucking sit the fuck down and shut up. Can you do that?

Shawn's pressuring of Tasha and friends worked. Tasha called the prosecutor's office to say that Shawn did *not* strangle her. Tasha recanted. She took back her statement. Tasha also didn't attend court proceedings.

DOI: 10.4324/9781003348696-1

However, a jury heard the recordings and recognized that Shawn had tampered with Tasha—that he had pressured her to say she lied to police about the abuse. Months before, Shawn had been convicted of strangling, physically assaulting, and raping Tasha. Strangulation is a major risk factor for repeat domestic violence and homicide (Campbell *et al.*, 2007) and is strongly linked to victim recantation (Kernic *et al.*, 2023).

Although the victim (Tasha) in this case is a woman and the abuser is a man (Shawn), domestic violence takes many forms, including female abusers against their male partners as well as same-sex domestic violence. However, criminally involved domestic violence cases (such as those that are the focus of our book) involve mostly male to female violence (80.5 percent) (McPhee *et al.*, 2022). Only 1.6 percent of criminally involved domestic violence cases involve same-sex violence (McPhee *et al.*, 2022).

Unfortunately, Tasha's experience is common. Domestic violence is a pervasive global problem impacting individuals, families, and communities (World Health Organization, 2021). Domestic violence can be life threatening, especially for female victims (Campbell *et al.*, 2007; Petrosky *et al.*, 2017; Stockl *et al.*, 2013). The World Health Organization (2021) estimates that almost one-third (27 percent) of women aged 15–49 years have been subjected to physical and/or sexual violence by their domestic partner. What is more, domestic violence was made worse by the novel coronavirus (COVID-19) pandemic and associated lockdowns—including escalating abuse, fewer services for victims, loss of jobs and household economic strain, and increased calls to police (Abu-Elenin *et al.*, 2022; Baidoo *et al.*, 2021; McCrary and Sanga, 2021; Nesset *et al.*, 2021; Roesch *et al.*, 2020).

What Is Recantation?

Recantation means to take back, withdraw, or repudiate formally and publicly a statement, opinion, or belief that has been made (Black's Law Dictionary, 2020). "To recant" is derived from two Latin roots: *re* meaning "back" and the verb *cantare* meaning "to sing" (Vocabulary.com).

In the field of domestic violence, recantation refers to victims who say they were abused and then take back or retract their statement. Prosecutors and advocates have known for many years that witness tampering is a significant problem in domestic violence cases and that victims recant and/or refuse prosecution due, in part, to perpetrators' threats of retaliation (Bennett *et al.*, 1999; Ellison, 2002; Hart, 1993; Meier, 2006). As recognized by the U.S. Supreme Court, "This particular type of crime is notoriously susceptible to intimidation or coercion of the victim to ensure she does not testify at trial" (*Davis v. Washington*, 126 S.Ct. 2266, 165 L Ed.2d 224, 2006). Subsequently, courts have empowered juries to consider the reality that "victims of domestic violence often attempt to placate their abusers in an effort to avoid repeated violence, and often minimize the degree of violence when discussing it with others" (for example, see *State v. Cook*, 131 Wn. App. 845, 129 P. 3d 834 [Div 2.2006]; *State v. Thach*, 126 Wn. App. 297, 307–08, 106 P. 3d 782 [2005]; and *State v. Bourgeois*, 133 Wn.2d 389, 945 P. 2d 1120 [1997]).

Recantation in domestic violence takes many forms. A victim might deny they were abused, say the abuse never happened, claim they lied and made up the abuse, allege misunderstanding or that the abuse was an "accident," or reattribute the violence, i.e., saying someone or something else was responsible. Recantation also commonly involves victims minimizing the impact of the abuse (e.g., "he just tugged at my hair") to lessen perceived severity (Bonomi *et al.*, 2011).

Victim recantation is widely depicted in news media through narratives about domestic violence. Highly publicized cases, such as the case involving victim Nicole Brown Simpson and her abuser O.J. Simpson (former National Football League star), fuel widespread victim-blaming narratives, i.e., that victims embody "unsavory" qualities (Zoglin, 1996). Public perceptions place added pressure on victims to keep their abusive relationship intact regardless of the personal costs to the victim (Patrick, 2018). Herein lies a paradox faced by victims: recant their story to protect themselves and preserve their emotional connection with their abuser, or possibly face further judgment.

Factors Associated With Recantation

For many years, research on factors leading to recantation focused on rich sources of data derived from case files and retrospective victim reports and interviews. This research partially linked victim recantation to threats and fear of retaliation (Cretney and Davis, 1997; Meier, 2006; Zoellner *et al.*, 2000), such as the previously mentioned case of Shawn threatening Tasha, though indirectly. Research also correlated victim nonparticipation in the prosecution process with the victim's financial dependence and cohabitation with the abuser (Camacho and Alarid, 2008; Ellison, 2002; Hart, 1993; McGuire *et al.*, 2021), the victim's belief that the crime is not severe enough to warrant prosecution (Hare, 2006), the victim's self-blame or embarrassment (McGuire *et al.*, 2021), the victim's substance abuse (Goodman *et al.*, 1999), the victim's perceptions of poor criminal justice response (e.g., dual arrest policies), and poor access to advocates and other social support systems (Bui, 2001; Cala *et al.*, 2016; Ellison, 2002; Hart, 1993).

In addition, domestic violence victims suffer elevated rates of clinical depression and anxiety (Bonomi *et al.*, 2009; Hegarty *et al.*, 2004), psychological trauma (Koepsell *et al.*, 2006), and traumatic brain injury (TBI) associated with memory loss, difficulty concentrating, blacking out, vision problems, ears ringing, hearing problems, dizzy spells, and seizures (Campbell *et al.*, 2018). Experiencing mental health–related symptoms and trauma, along with TBI specifically, could impact victims' ability to follow through with prosecution. However, it is important to note that victims can and do make decisions that protect themselves and loved ones, especially when supported by trauma-informed professionals.

Still yet, other factors may influence victims to recant and/or refuse prosecution. Victims are more likely to drop protection orders if concrete change (e.g., divorce/separation) or promised change (e.g., the abuser said he would change and get professional help) occurs (McGuire *et al.*, 2021; Roberts *et al.*, 2008), suggesting that victims' hope for change and their emotional attachments to their abuser motivate their decisions. This aligns with other studies linking emotional needs with continued involvement in abusive relationships (Allison *et al.*, 2008; Bartholomew and Allison, 2006; Cala *et al.*, 2016; Kernic *et al.*, 2023).

Kernic *et al.*'s study of 1,359 criminal cases showed that emotional connections, above other factors, were the strongest driver of recantation; victims who were dependent on the abuser for complex and intense emotional attachment or caretaking were 54 and 75 percent, respectively, more likely than other victims to recant or disengage from prosecution. Kernic *et al.*'s findings are consistent with Cala *et al.*'s 2016 findings that victims who remained in contact with their abuser or who had thoughts of getting back together were more likely than other victims to disengage from prosecution efforts. Also, Kernic *et al.'s* study found that victims who recanted or disengaged from prosecution were entrapped financially and partnered with abusers with more violent histories.

Abuser Tampering and Recantation

While the domestic violence field includes critical studies detailing factors associated with recantation, until the early 2000s, little was known about how domestic abusers tampered with their victims *in real time* to influence recantation. Researchers and prosecutors wondered: what were abusers saying, how were they saying it, and how did victims respond?

Some of those questions began to be answered in the early 2000s. For safety reasons, jails across the United States began recording all phone calls made from jail (except those involving attorney-client privilege). Recording jail calls came soon after a significant court decision that curtailed the ability of prosecutors to proceed without victim cooperation.

Coinciding with state privacy acts, calls made from jail came with warnings. Signs were posted in jails, and jail handbooks detailed that calls were "subject to recording" (Figure 1.1). In addition, all phone call participants heard a prerecorded message stating

Figure 1.1 Signs posted in jails warning that calls are recorded.

that their call would be recorded. Recipients of calls from jail had to click a button to indicate that they accepted that call with the understanding that their call would be recorded.

Despite these warnings, abusers still regularly called their victims from jail to pressure them to recant—often within hours of being arrested, some still intoxicated from alcohol and drug use. When abusers couldn't reach their victim directly, they called third parties (e.g., friends and family members, such as in the case of Shawn and Tasha), or they left voice messages for victims giving instructions and professing love. Abusers sometimes supplemented jail calls with text messages and handwritten letters.

In 2005, the first jail call involving a domestic violence case was recorded at the King County Detention Facility in Seattle's King County, Washington. We, the authors of this book, came together after this first recorded call about formally studying the jail calls to better understand both recantation and the dynamics of domestic violence.

After approval from the human subjects' ethics committee of the Ohio State University (Bonomi's academic institution), from 2008 to 2011, we listened to the jail calls of 25 couples involving a male abuser who had inflicted felony-level abuse against his female victim—the breakdown of 95 percent of cases reflected in the caseload of the King County Domestic Violence Unit. Felony-level domestic violence ranged from strangulation to physical assault resulting in injury (e.g., broken bones, lacerations, bruising) and the need for health services (e.g., emergency department visits, hospitalizations).

Details of our analysis of the jail calls from the 25 couples are described in Chapter 2. In brief, we concentrated on the following:

- Meeting weekly to discuss observations in the jail calls and capture notes and themes
- Writing narrative summaries of each jail call
- Developing a conceptual model
- Testing calls against the conceptual model to identify consistencies and exceptions to the rule (nuances to further strengthen the model)
- Presenting initial findings to research and practitioner audiences to collect their feedback

The result was a *five-stage model* of what domestic abusers say to their victims to influence recantation, how they say it, and how victims respond (Figure 1.2) (Bonomi *et al.*, 2011).

The *five-stage model* (with supporting jail-call examples) is detailed in Chapter 2. In brief, in *Stage 1*, the abuser and victim argued about the abuse event and mutual blame was cast, e.g., "I didn't push you down the stairs like you think I did!" In *Stage 2*, the abuser blamed the victim for the abuse and used "sympathy appeals" to position himself as the "victim" and manipulate the victim into feeling sorry for him. For example, the abuser reminded the victim of his impending jail sentence, the mental health problems he was experiencing (e.g., suicide risk), and his inability to be a good partner from behind bars. In *Stage 3*, the abuser and victim reminisced about earlier happier times and fear of what life would be like without one another. The abuser and victim positioned themselves "against others" (e.g., friends) for not understanding the specialness of their relationship. In *Stage 4*, the abuser asked the victim to recant, reinforced with sympathy appeals to position himself as the "victim." In *Stage 5*, once the victim "complied" with recanting (which the abuser had manipulated), the couple devised a plan. The plan included redefining the abuse to lessen its severity, positioning themselves against an "unfair" criminal justice system, and giving each other specific instructions on what to say in court (e.g., "Tell the judge you accidentally tripped me").

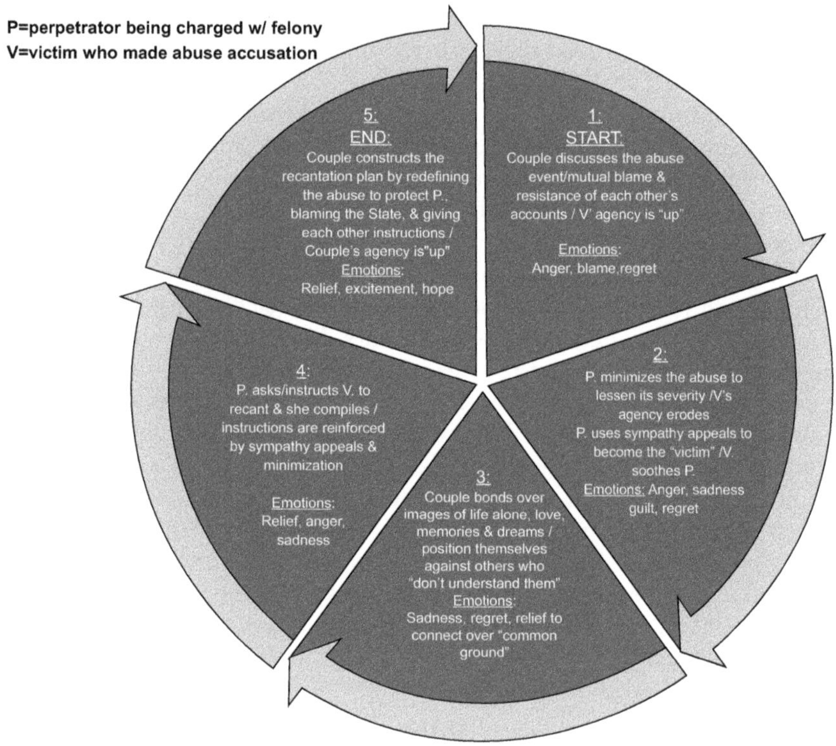

Figure 1.2 Five-stage model outlining how abusers tamper with their victims to influence recantation.
Source: From Bonomi *et al.*, 2011, reprinted with permission from Elsevier Publishers.

The *five-stage model* (Bonomi *et al.*, 2011) has been widely cited in legal opinions, amicus briefs, domestic violence manuals, and various places within the scientific community. Then, following training across the world with law enforcement, legal professionals, and health, social work, and emergency professionals, we published an extension of the *five-stage model* showing how abusers tamper with their family, friends, and children to influence victim recantation (Bonomi and Martin, 2018, 2020), and factors that trigger abuse in these couples (Nemeth *et al.*, 2012).

Goals of the Book

Despite uptake of the *five-stage model* in professional communities, to date, we have only reached a small fraction of professionals working in domestic violence. In fact, many professionals have shared with us that they have never listened to a jail call or been trained in the methods abusers use to pressure their victim to recant.

The principal goal of our book is to offer education on the precise interpersonal dynamics of recantation in criminal cases in which felony-level abuse has occurred. We put the reader directly in touch with what abusers say, how they say it, and how victims respond. Because our focus is on criminal cases and those involving felony-level abuse, what we discuss in the book might not apply to cases outside the criminal justice system and/or to cases involving less severe abuse.

- Chapter 2 details the *five-stage model* resulting from analyzing jail calls involving 25 couples.
- Chapter 3 summarizes the *five-stage model*, the limitations and strengths of our research, and areas for future investigation.
- Chapters 4 through 8 further detail the *five-stage model* using case examples supplemented with jail calls. These chapters include additional details about the case examples themselves, including contextual details about the abuse scene and the aftermath of recantation. The chapters also show how abusers triangulated third parties—friends and children—in the recantation process.
- Chapter 9 summarizes how the *five-stage model* advances an understanding of domestic violence and coercive control and emotional connection.
- Chapter 10 reviews professional applications using the *five-stage model* and jail calls to advance community response to domestic violence.

The jail recordings used in our book are official public records; the related legal matters have concluded. We have nonetheless undertaken extensive precautions to preserve the personal identities and safety of victims and abusers. We changed identifying details including names, dates, and key contextual information (e.g., locations, relationship details).

Readers of the print version of our book can access the jail recordings by visiting our website at: https://recantation.org/.

Our book is applicable to practitioners and research audiences in fields such as criminal law, family law, child custody, violence prevention, therapeutic interventions, medicine, nursing, psychology, social work, sociology, and behavioral economics.

We hope this book helps improve professional and community responses to domestic violence (Chapter 10), including advancing trauma-informed support for victims. We welcome input, feedback, ideas, and collaborations to advance work in this area.

References

Abu-Elenin, M.M., A.A. Elshora, M.S. Sadaka, and D.E. Abdeldaim. 2022. "Domestic violence against married women during the COVID-19 pandemic in Egypt." *BMC Women's Health* 22 (94).

Allison, C.J., K. Bartholomew, O. Mayseless, and D.G. Dutton. 2008. "Love as a battlefield: Dynamics in couples identified for male partner violence." *Journal of Family Issues* 20 (1): 125–150.

Baidoo, L., T.L. Zakrison, G. Feldmeth, S.T. Lindau, and E.L. Tung. 2021. "Domestic violence reporting and resources during the COVID-19 stay-at-home order in Chicago, Illinois." *JAMA Network Open* 4 (9): e2122260.

Bartholomew, K., and C.J. Allison. 2006. "An attachment perspective on abusive dynamics in intimate relationships." In *Dynamics of Romantic Love: Attachment, Caregiving, and Sex*, edited by M. Mikulincer and G.S. Goodman, 102–127. New York: Guilford.

Bennett, L., L. Goodman, and M. Dutton. 1999. "Systemic obstacles to the criminal prosecution of a battering partner." *Journal of Interpersonal Violence* 14 (7): 761.

Black's Law Dictionary, Free Online Legal Dictionary. (2020). Accessed November 28, 2022. http://thelawdictionary.org/recant/.

Bonomi, A.E., M.L. Anderson, R.J. Reid, F.P. Rivara, D. Carrell, and R.S. Thompson. 2009. "Medical and psychosocial diagnoses in women with a history of intimate partner violence." *Archives of Internal Medicine* 169 (18): 1692–1697.

Bonomi, A.E., R. Gangamma, C.R. Locke, H. Katafiasz, and D. Martin. 2011. "'Meet me at the hill where we used to park': Interpersonal processes associated with victim recantation." *Social Science and Medicine* 73: 1054–1061.

Bonomi, A.E., and D. Martin. 2018. "Jail calls: What do kids have to do with it." *Journal of Family Violence* 33 (2): 99–102.

Bonomi, A.E., and D. Martin. 2020. "Domestic abusers: Expert triangulators, new victim advocacy models to buffer against it." *Journal of Family Violence* 36: 383–388.

Bui, H.N. 2001. "Domestic violence victims' behavior in favor of prosecution effects of gender relations." *Women and Criminal Justice* 12 (4): 51–76.

Cala, M., M.E. Trigo, and F.J. Saavedra. 2016. "Women's disengagement from legal proceedings for intimate partner violence: Sociodemographic and psychological variables." *European Journal of Psychology Applied to Legal Context* 8: 35–42.

Camacho, C.M., and L.F. Alarid. 2008. "The significance of the victim advocate for domestic violence victims in municipal court." *Violence and Victims* 23 (3): 288–300.

Campbell, J.C., J.C. Anderson, A. McFadgion, J. Gill, E. Zink, M. Patch, G. Callwood, and D. Campbell. 2018. "The effects of intimate partner violence and probably traumatic brain injury on central nervous system symptoms." *Journal of Women's Health* 27 (6): 761–767.

Campbell, J.C., N. Glass, P.W. Sharps, K. Laughon, and T. Bloom. 2007. "Intimate partner homicide: Review and implications for research and policy." *Trauma, Violence and Abuse* 8 (3): 246–269.

Cretney, A., and G. Davis. 1997. "The significance of compellability in the prosecution of domestic violence cases." *British Journal of Criminology* 37: 75–89.

Ellison, L. 2002. "Prosecuting domestic violence without victim participation." *Modern Law Review* 65 (6): 834–858.

Goodman, L., L. Bennett, and M.A. Dutton. 1999. "Obstacles to victims' cooperation with the criminal prosecution of their abusers: The role of social support." *Violence and Victims* 14 (4): 427–444.

Hare, S.C. 2006. "What do battered women want? Victims' opinions on prosecution." *Violence and Victims* 21 (5): 611–628.

Hart, B. 1993. "Battered women and the criminal justice system." *American Behavioral Scientist* 36 (5): 624–638.

Hegarty, K., J. Gunn, P. Chondros, and R. Small. 2004. "Association between depression and abuse by partners of women attending general practice: Descriptive, cross-sectional survey." *British Medical Journal* 328: 621–624.

Kernic, M., L. Drolette, S. Shanahan, and D. Martin. 2023. *Victim Recantation and Disengagement from Prosecution in Intimate Partner Violence Criminally Prosecuted Crimes in King County.* Washington, DC: Predictors of Victim Recantation and Disengagement and Prosecutorial Outcomes. U.S. Department of Justice, National Institute of Justice (Grant #: 2017-VA-CX-0034).

Koepsell, J.K., M.A. Kernic, and V.L. Holt. 2006. "Factors that influence battered women to leave their abusive relationships." *Violence and Victims* 21 (2): 131–147.

McCrary, J., and S. Sanga. 2021. "The impact of the coronavirus lockdown on domestic violence." *American Law and Economics Review* 23 (1): 137–163.

McGuire, J., E. Evans, and E. Kane. 2021. "Victim and witness retraction and disengagement: A systematic review of contributing factors." In *Evidence-Based Policing and Community Crime Prevention*, 313–359. Advancing in Preventing and Treating Violence and Aggression. Cham: Springer.

McPhee, D., M. Hester, L. Bates, S.J. Lilley-Walker, and D. Patsios. 2022. "Criminal justice responses to domestic violence and abuse in England: An analysis of case attrition and inequalities using police data." *Policing and Society* 32 (8).

Meier, J.S. 2006. "*Davis/Hammon*, domestic violence, and the Supreme Court: The case for cautious optimism." *Michigan Law Review First Impressions* 22: 22–27.

Nemeth, J., A. Bonomi, M.A. Lee, and J.M. Ludwin. 2012. "Sexual infidelity as trigger for intimate partner violence." *Journal of Women's Health* 21 (9): 942–949.

Nesset, M.B., C.B. Gudde, G.E. Mentzoni, and T. Palmstierna. 2021. "Intimate partner violence during COVID-19 lockdown in Norway: The increase of police reports." *BMC Public Health* 21 (1): 2292.

Patrick, W.L. 2018. "How social stigma silences domestic violence victims." *Psychology Today*. https://www.psychologytoday.com/us/blog/why-bad-looks-good/201804/how-social-stigma-silences-domestic-violence-victims. Accessed November 28, 2022.

Petrosky, E., J.M. Blair, C.J. Betz, K.A. Fowler, S.P.D. Jack, and B.H. Lyons. 2017. "Racial and ethnic differences in homicides of adult women and the role of intimate partner violence—United States, 2003–2014." *Morbidity and Mortality Weekly Report* 66 (28): 741–746.

"Recant." *Vocabulary.com Dictionary*. Vocabulary.com, https://www.vocabulary.com/dictionary/recant. Accessed July 29, 2023.

Roberts, J.C., L. Wolfer, and M. Mele. 2008. "Why victims of intimate partner violence withdraw protection orders." *Journal of Family Violence* 23: 369–375.

Roesch, E., A. Amin, J. Gupta, and C. García-Moreno. 2020. "Violence against women during COVID-19 pandemic restrictions." *British Medical Journal* 369.

Stockl, H., K. Devries, A. Rotstein, N. Abrahams, J. Campbell, C. Watts, and C.G. Moreno. 2013. "The global prevalence of intimate partner homicide: A systematic review." *Lancet* 382 (9895): 859–865.

World Health Organization. 2021. *Violence against Women Prevalence Estimates, 2018: Global, Regional and National Prevalence Estimates for Intimate Partner Violence against Women and Global and Regional Prevalence Estimates for Non-partner Sexual Violence against Women*. Geneva: World Health Organization (Licence: CC BY-NC-SA 3.0 IGO).

Zoellner, L.A., N.C. Feeny, J. Alvarez, C. Watlington, M.L. O'Neill, R. Zager, and E.B. Foa. 2000. "Factors associated with completion of the restraining order process in female victims of partner violence." *Journal of Interpersonal Violence* 15 (10): 1081–1099.

Zoglin, R. 1996. "Blaming the victim: O.J. Simpson is back in court with a new defense strategy that aims to put his slain ex-wife on trial." *Time*, November 4. https://content.time.com/time/subscriber/article/0,33009,985425,00.html. Accessed November 28, 2022.

2 *Five-Stage Model of Recantation*

What Abusers Say, How They Say It, How Victims Respond

Jail-Call Study: An Analysis of Audio-Recorded Conversations

From 2008 to 2011, we analyzed jail calls between domestic abusers and their victims, recorded during the pre-prosecution period, to identify processes associated with victim recantation. Our analysis and study of the jail calls was approved by the Ohio State University's Institutional Review Board—the location of Dr. Bonomi's academic home. Subjects included 25 heterosexual couples, in which the male abuser was being held at the King County Detention Facility in Washington State for a felony-level domestic violence offense (e.g., assault, violation of a no-contact order, unlawful imprisonment) and made telephone calls from the facility to his victim (Figure 2.1). In 2005, the facility began routinely audio-recording telephone conversations of detainees to increase jail safety. All parties are aware they are being recorded through an automated message at

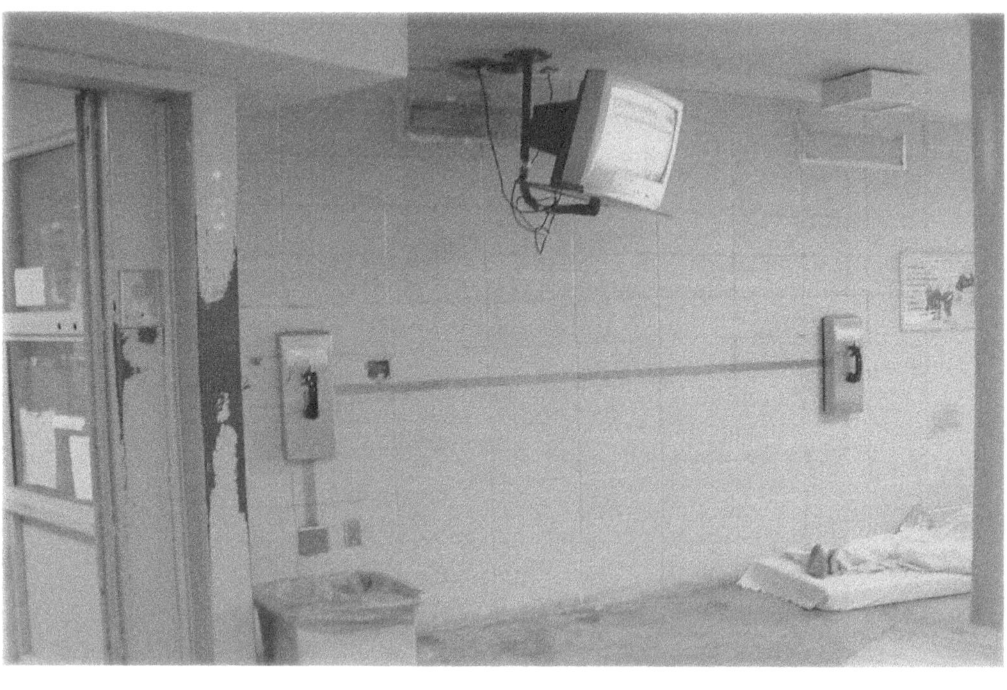

Figure 2.1 Phones used by abusers to call victims, King County Detention Facility, Seattle, Washington.

DOI: 10.4324/9781003348696-2

the beginning of each call. The legality of audio-recording telephone calls made from Washington State detention facilities was upheld in a Washington State Supreme Court decision (*State v. Modica*, 164 Wash.2d. 186 P. 3d 1062, Wash. July 10, 2008, NO. 79767–6). The prosecution division has authority to release the audiotapes for research purposes; tapes from 25 couples involved in felony-level domestic violence were provided to the study team for analysis. As the study involved secondary, public-record data, subjects were not required to provide informed consent.

Our sample size of 25 couples was chosen to ensure we achieved data saturation (the point where no new themes were identified) (Charmaz, 2006; Giacomini and Cook, 2000). We used 30–192 minutes of jail calls for each couple to explore two research questions: 1) What interpersonal processes were associated with the victim's intention to recant, including what was the couple discussing before and after it became clear that the victim would recant her story? That is, what were the abusers saying, how were they saying it, and how did the victims respond? 2) How did the couple construct the recantation plan once it was clear that the victim intended to recant?

We analyzed the jail calls using a rigorous, iterative approach that involved listening and relistening to calls, transcribing the calls, discussing the calls, and writing narrative summaries (Giacomini and Cook, 2000). We used constructivist grounded theory to guide data analysis, which allowed for the construction of a novel recantation framework (Charmaz, 2006), while simultaneously acknowledging the underlying coercive interpersonal dynamic whereby abusers manipulated conversations (Pence and Paymar, 1993) to influence victim recantation. The iterative analytic steps we used were as follows:

- From October to December 2008, the study team (Amy Bonomi [AB], Rashmi Gangamma [RG], Christopher Locke [CL], and Heather Katafiasz [HK]) met weekly to listen to the jail calls and compile notes.
- From January to July 2009, trained research assistants transcribed the jail calls of ten couples, where it was clear the victim intended to recant. The study team continued meeting weekly to review transcripts against the jail calls and to discuss emerging themes.
- From July to October 2009, AB and RG used the transcripts to write in-depth narrative summaries for the ten couples that addressed our two research questions, namely, what couples were discussing before and after it became clear the victim intended to recant and how couples then constructed the recantation plan (Figure 2.2 and Figure 2.3). The narrative summaries were reviewed iteratively with the study team and revised. Unlike many qualitative studies that use structured interviews to solicit themes, we were working with couples' raw, unstructured narratives; we therefore wrote narrative summaries of what couples were discussing instead of breaking the data into "code-able parts" to ensure continuity and integrity of the couples' narratives. Through November 2010, the preliminary findings were presented at six professional meetings and discussed with David Martin to test the credibility of the study team's interpretations.
- From this process, a conceptual framework (which became the *five-stage model*) was constructed and tested from September 2010 to June 2011. Testing the conceptual model involved extensive reengagement with the jail calls from the original ten couples, by rereading transcripts and reorganizing earlier themes. AB and RG then reviewed the jail calls of an additional 15 couples to confirm theoretical saturation (the point where no new themes were identified). The victim's intent to recant occurred in seven of the 15 additional couples, and they were added to the sample. In the remaining eight couples, the jail calls were not sufficiently audible or involved calls with the victim after a plea

bargain had been reached (still these calls involved victims who indicated an intent to recant). Since jail calls started to be recorded circa 2005, the quality of the technology for recording calls has improved significantly. In addition, since we published the jail-call study in 2011, through our prosecution and expert testimony work, we have compared the calls of many additional couples to the conceptual model to corroborate themes.

- Of the 17 couples that formed the focus of our study (the original ten couples plus the seven additional couples), the racial/ethnic makeup was as follows: Black (five couples), White (four couples), and mixed-race and/or unknown racial backgrounds (eight couples). All victims in our study had experienced felony-level violence, such as strangulation and physical assault.

Conversation 4: The conversation has a benign start with D asking E what she was doing. E sounds like she has a stuffy nose, which D makes note of. He tells that he has to go to court today for investigation of the assault. He wants to find out whether E filed a statement against him, but asks in an indirect way "*You think I'm getting' out*?" E informs him that he could if they don't hold him against the no-contact order. D wants to know how they found out about the no-contact order. E reiterates that she did not file a report and that she *"walked away"* when the cops asked her questions. The next few minutes they talk about what's probably going to happen to him and the nature of charges that could be pressed against him. D becomes increasingly agitated in this part of the conversation. He then asks, in what seems to be an attempt to draw her into a conversation about their relationship, *"So what do you* want *me to do, just leave or just-just disappear or something*'?" E says that that would probably be the best thing for him and that she's cleaning up her room for a reason. She also says - *"I just can't do it any more"*. (I am leaving you). At this point D becomes very agitated (perceived threat of loss) and reacts by accusing her of being responsible for everything that's happening to him. (Blame the victim) He says that she wants to bring him down and keep him down and blames her even for the violent incident. He raises his voice, talks over her, and repeats words and sentences and keeps interrupting E when she tries to speak. E initially seems to accept her part (*"I know exactly what* it is. *It's just* me.."), but this seems more an attempt to not get into the argument rather than an acceptance of blame. She tries to tell him that they are not going to work and attempts to counter his accusation. But she is unable to get more than a few words across to him (It does not seem like D is listening because he is extremely upset). D says that E could have left the club (the scene of the last violent incident) because he gave her keys to the car. He accuses her of "aggravating" the situation even when she knew he has an "anger problem". (Blame the victim) D also says that he has been working hard but has nothing to show for it, that he has been trying to help her, but she wants him down. (Appeal to victim's sympathy) The theme in his argument is that he is the victim: He was just trying to have fun on a Friday night but she followed him to the club and aggravated him; he gave her keys to leave but she wouldn't, and also he broke her nose, because she wanted him to do that. So, it appears that he believes she is against him and he is somehow the victim because nobody gives him a chance to do better. Even in this brief exchange, as soon as E suggests that she is done, he becomes extremely agitated and lashes out. In this exchange, both D and E say they are leaving. E says that directly, *"I just can't do it anymore"*, and D says it more indirectly "I'm *'bout to get off the phone man"* (interestingly, this is just before he lashes out), and *"bye man"*, but neither actually hangs up and the conversation continues till the end of the allotted time. E states multiple times that D will be alright. It appears that she wants to reassure him that he will be okay and that it's okay for her to leave. She even alludes to involvement of other women in his life (*"you'll be alright, D, and um you will, everybody vill wanna fuck wit you, all the bitches that liked you, remember*?"). It may be an attempt to reduce her own guilt for talking about leaving him. D's brother is apparently also in jail (maybe in the same place) and she asks him not to worry ....

Figure 2.2 Sample narrative summary.

Conversation 2: In this conversation, the perpetrator uses numerous tactics to appeal to the victim's sympathy, for example, he cries at several points (including in the opening lines), calls up the painful loss of his son if he were to do jail time, calls up the intolerable idea of being in prison ("in the hole") for sixty to ninety days, and calls up the immediate dire setting of the jail ("I've been in the hole for five days... fuck, I haven't taken a shower in three days"). Interestingly, he does not bring up the idea that losing their relationship would be painful - although at one point when the couple is discussing the involvement of CPS and the victim's mother's desire for her to get a paternity test, the perpetrator appears threatened and responds: *I'm not gonna leave you.* Instead of focusing on fostering his relationship with the victim, the perpetrator wants the victim to do jail time to alleviate his suffering. The couple forges closeness over multiple topics: the perpetrator's emotional state (he's having anxiety attacks in jail and also cries at several points during the conversation), their special connection *(nobody knows I'm in jail but you)*, what the victim is going to say/do in jail to lessen charges, their son, their feelings towards supporting witnesses (the victim's friend is triangulated because her story will support prosecution of the perpetrator), their feelings toward the state (the perpetrator says: *We'll blow her up* (the prosecutor) up tomorrow / victim follows: *Okay*, I'm *gonna ask her how many time-if what-if I made the whole thing up* and their communication mechanisms (they are distraught that they haven't been able to reach each other by phone, and bond late in the conversation over the "smell" of a letter the victim wrote (*This smells like it's from Victoria's Secret*). Even in situations of disagreement, such as what happened during the violent event, the couple is actively engaged with each other. The conversation opens with the anxious and threatened demeanor of the perpetrator, who is crying because he hasn't been able to get a hold of the victim by phone. The conversation immediately shifts, with the perpetrator telling the victim that he's going to the Supreme Court and that the victim needs to be in court to tell the judge that what she wrote on the police report was a lie (*"that way ... somethin' you said*" and "*I'll get off scot-free"*); the bulk of the conversation is then spent scheming what the victim will say in order to lessen the perpetrator's charges (*You've just gotta say that what you wrote in the statement is a lie, that you're mad at me cause you thought I was cheatin on you with your cousin .....*) / Victim (laughing): *OK/ If you say that, they'll automatically let me go* / Victim: *OK*/ Perp: *You know I love you?* (pursuit) / (Later on in the conversation, the perpetrator returns to the theme of the victim's big mouth: "*Sometimes ya got a big mouth, and that's how I got* into *this situation.*" This is a continuation from the first conversation, where the perpetrator says the victim had to *call police like* a *bitch)*. The victim agrees and the perpetrator immediately asks to talk to "my son" (Another plea to her sympathy, also anxiety about abandonment). The couple forges closeness over talking about how much the son misses his daddy. The perpetrator then tells the victim he had an anxiety attack and was placed in the psych ward ("*I just freaked out, man.* The couple triangulates C, a friend of the victim who will testify against the perpetrator if she comes to court; the couple agrees that C shouldn't be at court, which is interesting b/c she is otherwise a close friend of the victim *(You can't bring C cause she's part of the* whole *deal* too / OK). (Interpretation: don't bring C b/c she will tell the WHOLE TRUTHFUL STORY.) LATER ON, the couple returns to tactics the victim will take to do time for the perpetrator: Perpetrator: *Cause like, you know, they might give you five or ten days but that's better than me doing sixty to ninety* / Me? / Perpetrator: *Yah, but that's better than me doing sixty to ninety / FUCK ... I don't wanna go to jail for five days* Perp: *Babe, I just spent five days in the hole. You can't do five days for me? Would you rather me sit* in *her for sixty to ninety? ...*

Figure 2.3 Sample narrative summary.

Results of Our Analysis of the Jail Calls

Figure 1.2 depicts the *five-stage model* that emerged from our analysis of the jail calls. The processes associated with a victim's intent to recant did not unfold linearly. Starting at the top of Figure 1.2, *Stage 1*, the couple's early conversations typically included an argument about what transpired during the abuse event and/or what led up to it. In these early conversations, abusers and victims acted as "separate" individuals and expressed anger, blame, and resistance of each other's accounts of what happened. Initially, victims exercised agency (self-determination) by "telling the truth about what happened" and even calling the abuser an "abuser." However, the victim's agency was fleeting, unraveling in response to three processes that were also associated with her intention to recant

(*Stages 2 and 3*): the abuser's minimization of the abuse event, the abuser's appeals to her sympathy (the "tipping point" for influencing recantation), and the couple's expressed need to keep their relationship and family intact. Minimization of the abuse and appealing to the victim's sympathy occurred early in the conversations, but importantly, these strategies also continued in various forms, even after the victim indicated her intention to recant. In the later stages of the model (*Stages 4 and 5*), typically the abuser made a direct request for the victim to recant reinforced with sympathy appeals followed by the couple working together on what they would say in court; while working together, the couple assumed the role of "couple" united against the judicial process (*Stage 5*). We labeled the segments in Figure 1.2 with numerical values to aid readers in moving through the various sections. However, as will be described, couples did not necessarily move through the phases linearly. In addition, as will be described in later chapters, sometimes couples cycled through several stages of the model within a 30-second interaction, only to circle back through the stages again. Following, we describe each of the stages in the *five-stage model* in detail, supported with audio-recordings.

Stage 1: Discussion (and Minimization) of the Abuse Event

In *Stage 1*, couples argued over what happened before, during, and after the abuse event. In these early conversations, abusers and victims expressed anger and blame and resisted each other's accounts of what happened. At first, victims called out the abusers' bad behavior, exercising agency and self-determination. However, the victims' determination to hold the abusers accountable eroded under the abusers' persistent minimization of the abuse and discrediting of the victims. While abusers' minimization of the abuse event did not serve as the tipping point for prompting victims to recant their stories, repeated use of minimization effectively served to lessen the victims' perceptions of the severity of the crime and wear down the victims' agency. Abusers' use of minimization included the following:

- Silencing the victim from talking about abuse
- Resisting responsibility for the abuse
- Questioning the credibility of the victim's story
- Blaming the victim for the abuse

For example, one victim confronted her abuser after being severely beaten. In response, her abuser insisted that the victim provoked the abuse:

Victim: Why are you constantly beating on me, though?
Abuser: I'm not constantly beating on you . . . you, you don't understand that you beat on me with words and I can't defend myself.
Victim: With words, but I don't hit you.
Abuser: Hit me, you hit me so fuckin' hard mentally, I'm a very fragile person . . . mentally.
Victim: I would, I would um rather be verbally attacked.
Abuser: I would never want to be verbally attacked in my state, it's always a defense and then me taking it to the point where you get my level going over the flipside and I lose it like the Incredible Hulk.

In another couple, the victim screamed at her abuser that her cheek was broken. The abuser disregarded her broken cheek and attributed her injury to "the door."

Victim: My face is fucked up, I don't know how I'm gonna go to work (long pause). I've gotta go in there looking like shit.
Abuser: The whole side? [of your face]
Victim: The whole side of my face. (long pause) I mean, you hit me, I can't even tell you how hard you hit me. And it went right on the cheekbone so it went everywhere.
Abuser: That was (sigh) the door [that broke your cheekbone].
Victim: It wasn't the door, it wasn't the door, it was a fist.
Abuser: Nevermind, nevermind, nevermind, you're just gonna have it your way . . . I don't wanna argue.
Victim: It wasn't anything to do with the door!
Abuser: Okay, okay, okay, man . . . you gonna stay fixated on that too? This ain't gonna work. I'm fucked . . . for life. Shit.

Stage 2: Appeals to the Victim's Sympathy

Of all processes associated with the victim's intention to recant, most significant were the abuser's appeals to the victim's sympathy through descriptions of his suffering. Even victims who were "holding their own" against the abuser's resistance of responsibility were vulnerable to the abuser's accounts of personal suffering. Following such accounts, victims who seemed intent on following through with prosecution efforts began to change their stance, moving from a space of anger and resistance to sadness, guilt, and regret and attempted to soothe the abuser (*Stage 2*). In describing suffering, abusers expressed an increase in depression and anxiety symptoms, which reversed the roles in the couple's relationship, with the abuser becoming a "victim" of his suffering and the victim becoming his caretaker. In one case, the victim initially refused to help the abuser and even threatened to talk to the police about previous incidents of violence. However, her stance softened when the abuser became increasingly anxious and threatened suicide. He screamed: "You're making me go crazy. They're telling me they're gonna press charges then, damn. You wanna see a motherfucker suicidal?" His panic was evident as the victim continued to threaten him with pressing charges. Finally, he asked in a distressed tone: "Can I say goodbye? Can I say something? Nobody loves me though, right?" This was a crucial point where the victim's tone changed drastically; she sounded concerned he may actually do something to himself. The remaining conversations revolved around the victim trying to assuage the abuser's anxiety and promising to do her best to help him get out of jail.

In another example, the abuser described suffering from anxiety and depression and needing to spend time in the psych ward in the jail. In response to the abuser's insinuations of suicide, the victim attempted to soothe the abuser by reminding him she was at home thinking about him.

Abuser: I don't want to be here. (crying, sniffling)
Victim: I know, baby. (baby cooing in the background) How is it? Is it really, really bad in there?

Abuser: Hell bad. Ah, ah, that's why I haven't been able to call you. I broke down yesterday, I had a fuckin' had a fuckin' anxiety attack yesterday and they put me in the psych ward.
Victim: What is a psych ward? What does that mean?
Abuser: Psych ward? Where suicide people go. (distressed)
Victim: So you're trying to kill yourself?! (worried)
Abuser: No [distressed tone]. I just freaked out, man, waking up in the same hole, I mean, without being able to talk to my family.
Victim: Awe, awe, I'm thinkin' about you, I'm home.

Other powerful appeals to the victim's sympathy involved describing suffering due to life without the victim and their children. One abuser began a call distraught, telling the victim, "Oh my god, I love you. I haven't been able to call you." He then immediately instructed the victim to recant: "I'm goin' to the Supreme Court. you gotta be there, you gotta sit up front and tell them that what you wrote in the (police) report was a lie." The victim responded: "Uh-huh, I will." He continued the sympathy appeal with, "Oh my god, let me talk to my son. Hi, baby. I don't wanna be here." Most abusers and victims repeatedly invoked their roles as partners and parents to remind each other of what they stood to lose if prosecution moved forward. One abuser reminded the victim that their child was crying: "Cause her daddy ain't here. She's sad her daddy's gone. That's all that is. She's sensing her daddy ain't there. She's sensing something is wrong."

Stage 3: Connecting Over Common Ground

The victim's recantation intention was also associated with the couple invoking images of life without each other and bonding over love, dreams, and memories. The couple invoking images of life without each other and bonding over shared similarities typically occurred after the couple had argued about what happened during the abuse event and after the abuser used sympathy appeals; however, for some couples, images of life without each other were invoked early in the conversations.

When reminding each other of life alone and/or bonding over love, dreams, and memories, both the abuser and victim tended to express sadness and regret but also relief that they were connecting over common ground. In one couple, the victim played the couple's "theme song"; the song's refrain (Stay or leave/I want you not to go/But you did) reinforced the tenuousness of their relationship posed by the abuser's jail time. In response, the abuser cried and invoked an image of their earlier connection: "There is our song (sniffling, crying), it reminds me of our time at the spa." The victim added: "I could feel your spirit moving with the song." Similarly, other couples invoked images of special places they used to meet to share romantic moments (e.g., "Meet me at the hill where we used to park"), symbolizing a desire to meet each other halfway during the telephone conversations to get the abuser out of jail to resume their in-person connection.

Still yet, other couples used religious imagery to solidify their connection: "Listen to me, this is your husband talking to you, the Buddha [religious reference] said we both need to listen to each other, right? That's really important to me because I'm hurting right now [sympathy appeal]. I'm hurting right now because we don't listen to each other . . . but if we start listening to each other . . . from this point on, I'd like ask that we start acting like husband and wife" [image of solid connection]. The victim agreed that they should heed Buddha's advice and listen to each other.

In some couples, the need to keep their relationship and family intact was discussed in the context of others' opposition of their relationship. Couples believed that they shared a unique bond not understood by others. For instance, in one couple, where their families expressed displeasure over the relationship, the abuser used this to reinforce his dedication to the victim and their family: "She (his mom) was like, 'don't be calling (the victim) . . . do you want to be with her?' . . . I was like, fuck yeah, she's got my fucking daughter." When the victim suggested they get tattoos of their full name on each other's neck to prove their commitment, he said: "If I get a tattoo with your name, my mom is gonna kick my ass. My grandma, my family is gonna kick my ass . . . I'll get your name, as long as you get my name."

In one couple, after the abuser had raped his girlfriend, he interchanged sympathy appeals ("I read the cards wrong") with professing that the act of sex (rape) was an act toward marriage and giving his girlfriend the daughter she had always wanted.

Abuser: (sigh) I read the cards wrong.
Victim: What? (angry)
Abuser: I must have read the cards wrong.
Victim: No shit.
Abuser: (inaudible) after a fight, we could make love . . . and . . . maybe there'd be a chance for you to conceive the daughter that you wanted . . . and our relationship would work and we'd end up married with kids.

To further solidify an emotional connection, abusers supplemented jail calls with handwritten letters (Figure 2.4). In Figure 2.4, an abuser's letter began with, "I wish that you

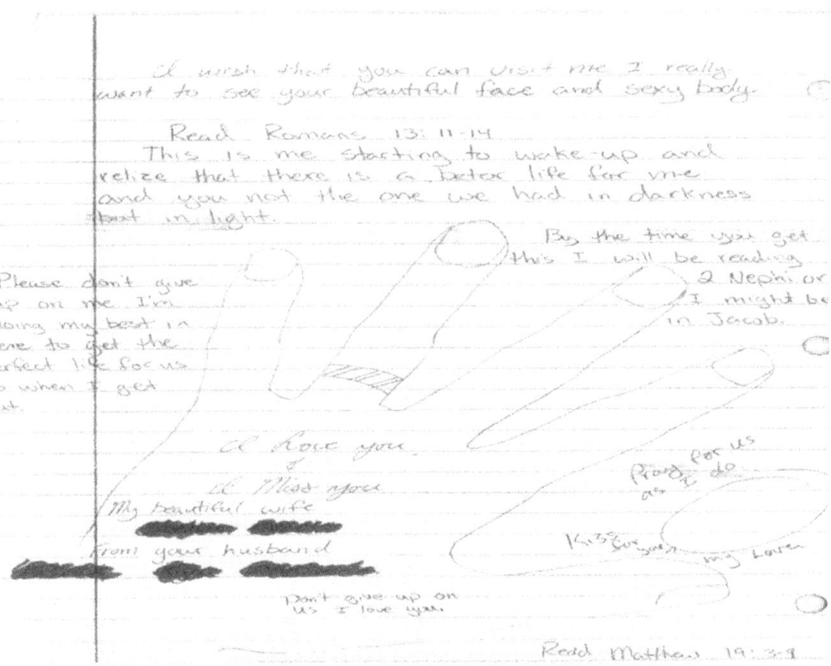
I wish that you can visit me I really want to see your beautiful face and sexy body.

Read Romans 13: 11-14
This is me starting to wake-up and relize that there is a betor life for me and you not the one we had in darkness but in light.

By the time you get this I will be reading 2 Nephi or I might be in Jacob.

Please don't give up on me I'm doing my best in here to get the perfect life for us so when I get out.

I Love you
&
I Miss you
My beautiful wife
From your husband

Don't give up on us I love you.

Pray for us as I do

Kiss for you my Love

Read Matthew 19: 3-9

Figure 2.4 Letter written from jail.

can visit me. I really want to see your beautiful face and sexy body." The abuser had strangled the victim and broken several facial bones. The abuser drew the outline of his hand with a wedding band on his ring finger and referenced "my beautiful wife" even though the couple were not married. The strategy of referring to "husband" and "wife" conjured the idea of a solid connection and held out the promise of marriage. Promises of rehabilitation added to the abuser's attempts to show dedication to the victim.

Stages 4 and 5: Recantation Request and Instructions

Again, while the process within couples did not unfold linearly, once couples processed the early phases of anger over differing accounts of what happened, sympathy appeals, and bonding over love, dreams, and memories, the victim moved into a place of stating her intention to recant. Typically, the victim's recantation intention was prompted by the abuser asking or instructing them to recant. When it was clear the victim intended to recant, both members of the couple tended to express relief and renewed energy as they went about constructing the recantation plan; as well, in some couples, hope of better times in the future was an expressed feeling. Importantly, for many couples in this phase, both members of the couple moved from foremost representing themselves as "individuals" and instead representing themselves as a "united couple."

Three strategies were typically used in constructing the plan: redefining the abuse event to protect the abuser; blaming the State (i.e., the criminal justice system) for the couple's separation; and exchanging specific instructions on what should be said or done in court or when interacting with other legal representatives or family members and friends before the abuser's appearance in court.

Redefining the Abuse Narrative

By the time the victim intended to recant, the abuser's repetitious minimization of the abuse event and resistance of responsibility influenced the victim into adopting a modified account of what happened. Redefining the abuse narrative involved continuing to minimize the severe violence and injuries that the victim sustained and redefining their roles in the violent dispute.

In one couple, what started as the abuser planning to tell the judge that he did not "even touch" the victim turned into plans to tell the judge that he was "in a blackout" and "needs anger management." The initiative as to what to tell the judge was led by the victim.

Abuser: I will see what the judge has to say and I'm gonna say what I have to say but pretty much I'm, I'm going to stick with my story . . . I, I didn't even touch you.

Victim: I wouldn't do that because then you're lying . . . be up front, be like "I was out of control drunk, I was in a blackout. I would normally, I would've never done something like that."

Abuser: And that I, I need anger management, I need to start going to classes, I need to request days off to go to anger management? NO!

Victim: But you need to tell the judge that you do need [anger management] . . . so they let you the fuck out of there . . . otherwise they're going to keep you in there.

Here, the victim exercised her own agency in helping to establish the plan of how to minimize the abuser's actions. However, the couple's agency ultimately prevailed through the uniting over a common purpose to help the abuser get out of jail.

Blaming the State

Couples typically perceived the State as a common enemy by the time the victim intended to recant, a persecuting agency that did not recognize the specialness of their relationship. In the arrest aftermath, the couples resolved to preserve their special connection; recantation was an important step toward this preservation. One victim exemplified blaming the State in breaking up the couple's relationship:

> I told the judge we don't want it, they're ruining people's lives. (The) domestic violence advocate called me, she said the whole case is totally unfair and I told her what happened and she said that no-contact order is totally not fair because we didn't want it, we do not want it . . . we want to be together and have a family, we have children.

In another couple, as the abuser and victim were constructing the recantation plan, the abuser enthusiastically suggested, "We'll blow her (the prosecutor) up tomorrow" to which the victim responded by engaging in discussion about what they will say in court. While our data did not consistently show that victims questioned the credibility of the justice system, one victim involved with her abuser for nearly 20 years vocalized her anger and disappointment in the judicial system: "You get a slap on the wrist, that's it and then you're out (of jail)."

Exchanging Instructions on What Should Be Said or Done

Abusers and victims both offered instructions on what should be said or done in court, with abusers often coupling such instructions with proclamations of care for the victim and with sympathy appeals.

In one couple, the abuser instructed his victim to say she lied to police so that she would serve jail time instead of him, reinforcing his instructions with a sympathy appeal.

Abuser: Oh my god, I love you . . . I haven't been able to call you (crying) . . . Alright I gotta tell you somethin' . . . um, I'm goin' to the Supreme Court, but you gotta be there . . . you gotta sit up front and you gotta tell 'em that . . . what you wrote on, in uh the police report was a lie, that you're just mad at me 'cause you thought I was cheatin' on you with your cousin. If you say that—

Victim: (Laughs) Okay.

Abuser: If you say that, they'll automatically let me go.

Victim: Okay.

Abuser: Alright?

Victim: Uh-huh.

Abuser: You know I love you? . . . Cause like, you know, but they might give you five or ten days, but that's better than me doing 60–90 days.

Victim: Me?!

Abuser: Yeah, but, babe, that's better than me doing 60–90 days . . . they probably give you five days for filing a false police report, that's it.
Victim: I don't want to go to jail for five days. (distressed)
Abuser: Babe, I just spent five days in the hole. You can't do five days for me?

Conclusions

We used recorded jail calls, and a rigorous qualitative analysis, to describe interpersonal processes associated with a victim's intention to recant. A victim's recantation intention was influenced by the abuser's minimization of the abuse and appeals to her sympathy through descriptions of his suffering from mental and physical problems, intolerable jail conditions, and life without her. The intention was further solidified by the couple invoking images of life without each other and bonding over love, dreams, and memories. Once the victim arrived at her intention to recant, the couple constructed the recantation plan by redefining the abuse event to protect the abuser, blaming the State for the couple's separation, and exchanging specific instructions on what should be said or done.

In our study, direct threats were rarely used to influence victims; in only one couple did the abuser directly threaten the victim: "If you go against me on this one, it's gonna be the worst mistake you ever make in your whole life." While the threat of further violence was present in all couples, the detained abusers in our study used other sophisticated strategies to persuade their victim, namely, minimization and descriptions of their suffering; these strategies successfully triggered sadness, guilt, and sympathy in their victim, which served to strengthen the case for changing her story to protect him. Despite abusers' persuasion, our results also point to the victim's expressed desire to keep the relationship intact and strategies the couple used to shape the recantation plan; for example, by blaming the State, the couple assumed the united role as "victim" against an "unfair judicial process."

References

Bonomi, A.E., R. Gangamma, C.R. Locke, H. Katafiasz, and D. Martin. 2011. "'Meet me at the hill where we used to park': Interpersonal processes associated with victim recantation." *Social Science and Medicine* 73: 1054–1061.

Charmaz, K. 2006. *Constructing Grounded Theory: A Practical Guide Through Qualitative Analysis*. London: Sage Publications.

Giacomini, M.K., and D.J. Cook. 2000. "Users' guide to the medical literature XXIII. Qualitative research in health care. A. Are the results valid?" *Journal of the American Medical Association* 284 (3): 357–362.

Pence, E., and M. Paymar. 1993. *Education Groups for Men Who Batter: The Duluth Model*. New York: Springer Publishing Company.

3 Recapping the *Five-Stage Model*

Its Limitations and Strengths

Recapping the *Five-Stage Model*

Our results from Bonomi *et al.* (2011) (i.e., the *five-stage model* of recantation) support that witness tampering is a significant problem in domestic violence cases. To recap, the *five-stage model* illustrates that a victim's recantation intention was influenced by the abuser's minimization of the abuse and appeals to her sympathy through descriptions of his suffering from mental and physical problems, intolerable jail conditions, and life without her. The intention was further solidified by the couple invoking images of life without each other and bonding over love, dreams, and memories. Once the victim arrived at her intention to recant, the couple constructed the recantation plan by redefining the abuse event to protect the abuser, blaming the State for the couple's separation, and exchanging specific instructions on what should be said or done.

Direct threats of inflicting future violence were rarely used to influence victims; in only one couple did the abuser directly threaten the victim saying, "If you go against me on this one, it's gonna be the worst mistake you ever make in your whole life." While the threat of further violence and assault was present in all couples, the detained abusers in our study used other sophisticated strategies to persuade their victim, namely, minimization (Pence and Paymar, 1993) and descriptions of their suffering. These strategies successfully triggered sadness, guilt, and sympathy in their victim, which served to strengthen the case for changing her story to protect him.

Despite abusers' persuasiveness, our results also point to the victim's expressed desire to keep the relationship intact but for the abuse to stop, as illustrated here:

Victim: Well, we have to stop that [fighting with each other].
Abuser: Yeah you do.
Victim: We, we—
Abuser: You do, you do, you do.
Victim: If it can't be "we" then we're not gonna make it.
Abuser: There ain't no first class here, there ain't no we.
Victim: It's not funny.
Abuser: We, we. Alright? We.
Victim: I love you and stop being mean.
Abuser: We. Okay, we.
Victim: I love you.
Abuser: I love you too.

DOI: 10.4324/9781003348696-3

This sequence was followed by the victim saying, "I love you so much I wish you were home I miss you," followed by the abuser's retort, "Yeah don't even start with that shit cause it's gonna be a really long time." The abuser then told the victim she could go to the court and "I don't know—try somethin'." After a series of I love you's near the end of the conversation, the abuser complained that his back hurt—which drew attention to himself and engaged the victim's need to care for him.

Limitations of Our Study and the *Five-Stage Model*

The goal of our analysis of the jail calls (culminating in the *five-stage model*) is to describe a particular phenomenon: recantation processes in couples with felony-level domestic violence offenses. Our findings therefore reflect processes in couples with severe rather than less severe violence. It is possible that different processes play out in couples with less severe violence; additional research would need to be conducted to examine this topic. Also, we did not analyze jail calls in which the victim did not indicate an intention to recant. With additional resources, future studies must examine recordings between victim and abuser in situations where the victim does not express her intention to recant—to examine whether differences in interactional patterns exist and how these differences could inform practice.

Our *five-stage model* could not fully detail all contextual factors previously shown through victim interviews and case file reviews to be associated with recantation, such as financial stress, children, substance abuse, disillusionment with the judicial system, and concrete and promised changes (e.g., Bui, 2001; Camacho and Alarid, 2008; Ellison, 2002; Hart, 1993; Roberts *et al.*, 2008). Rather, our use of jail calls allowed for the construction of a novel recantation framework that addressed real-time interpersonal processes associated with a victim's intention to recant.

Nonetheless, the recantation processes identified in the *five-stage model* must be considered within the larger context of the couple's relational situation, including those factors previously shown to be associated with victim nonparticipation in the prosecution process. For example, while the principal factors associated with victim recantation identified in our study included minimization, sympathy appeals, and the couple's shared desire to stay together, some couples discussed financial troubles as a factor previously shown to motivate victims to recant (Camacho and Alarid, 2008; Ellison, 2002; Hart, 1993). In our study, financial troubles were not specifically discussed in relation to recantation but could have been a motivating factor for the victim taking back her story. Interviews with victims would be needed to answer this question. As well, many couples in our sample had children; however, while only one victim identified her child's needs as a motivation for recanting, other victims could have been internally processing their children's needs; interviews with victims would help clarify their desires and motivations. Finally, except for one victim, across our sample in Bonomi *et al.* 2011, victims did not express disillusionment with the judicial system; that disillusioned victim had been involved with her abuser for nearly 20 years and expressed frustration that her abuser simply got a "slap on the wrist" each time he perpetrated severe violence. Disillusionment with the judicial process could be explored further in future research.

In addition to possible motivations related to children, finances, and disillusionment with the criminal justice system, prior research has shown a relationship between having access to tangible support and victim participation in the prosecution process (Cala *et al.*, 2016; Dawson and Dinovitzer, 2001; Goodman *et al.*, 1999). Although we did not set out to explore the role of formal or informal support in influencing victim recantation behavior, we did observe that when the victims in our jail-call study were in the presence of supportive others (e.g., friends and/or family members) while talking to their abuser, their agency and resistance to their abuser appeared to be greater. This was the case for several victims whose family members and/or friends were present during a portion of their conversations with the incarcerated abuser. Although the presence of others did not ultimately change victims' actions in our study, victims appeared better able to resist the persuasion of the abuser when they had support.

Strengths and Implications of Our Study and the *Five-Stage Model*

Our jail-call study advances knowledge about strategies abusers used (e.g., sympathy appeals and minimization) to persuade their victims and strategies the couple used (e.g., bonding against others who did not understand their relationship) to preserve their relationship.

Our study findings point to the need for recantation frameworks that recognize both the abuser's behavioral tactics and two other critical relationship processes, as follows:

1. The needs and desires of the victim in maintaining the relationship, even though the relationship would possibly be deemed by others (e.g., friends, family members, law enforcement) as "harmful" and/or "unhealthy." It is common for people in any interpersonal relationship (violent or not) to be invested in maintaining their relationship for a variety of reasons (e.g., children, interconnected families, business interests, love, familiarity). Many victims deeply love their partners and want the relationship to work, but they want the abuse to stop and do not know how and are often not able to stop the abuse. An abuser's manipulation of the victim is so successful in part because they are pressuring the victim to engage in normative behavior (to remain in and maintain the relationship) even though the relationship is characterized by significant harm. Recognition of the victim's needs and desires ensures the victim's agency is acknowledged in the pathways and outcome of their relationships. This recommendation is not at odds with the other work acknowledging and prioritizing victim needs.
2. The interplay of emotions in couples in which violence occurs. Specifically, the abuser's use of sympathy appeals through descriptions of his suffering from mental and physical problems, intolerable jail conditions, and impending life without the victim and their children was a highly successful tactic in manipulating the victim's emotional state, shifting her from a place of maintaining her agency in moving forward with prosecution to resuming caretaking of the abuser. The sympathy appeals used by abusers were typically accompanied by displays of their distressed emotional state (e.g., anxious, sad), and such appeals augmented the abuser's power over the victim's emotional state; thus, upon hearing the abuser's distressed plea for help, the victim responded by helping lessen his anxiety.

Our work underscores that the abusive interpersonal dynamic that existed before the arrest continued while abusers were in detention. Further, the continued use of abusive strategies by abusers is well documented in the literature (e.g., manipulation involving minimization of the abuse) (Allison *et al.*, 2008; Pence and Paymar, 1993) along with other sophisticated emotional manipulation (e.g., sympathy appeals) to erode victim's agency and achieve the abuser's goal of getting out of jail. Like the Roberts *et al.* (2008) study and prior studies focused on the connection between emotional needs and abuse patterns (Allison *et al.*, 2008; Kernic *et al.*, 2023), the victims and abusers in our study were motivated by emotional attachment to each other.

Our expanded conceptualization of recantation has been used to train judges, law enforcement personnel, victim advocates, and other professionals (e.g., social workers) to recognize not just the threats but also the complex interpersonal processes including sympathy appeals and minimization of the abuse, which serve to keep violent relationships intact. Our conceptualization is not at odds with training that is currently done in some law enforcement and clinical settings, in which service providers are instructed to put aside their own biases about what they believe the victim "should do" and instead focus on the victim's needs and desires.

Our findings also point to the importance of providing supportive assistance to victims (Goodman *et al.*, 1999), including having a trusted victim advocate or similar representative work with victims early on and throughout the criminal justice process. This support can defend against the sophisticated techniques that abusers use. Victim advocates have shared with us that when they used the *five-stage model* to forewarn victims on what to expect—that their abuser will use sympathy appeals, for example—victims appreciated being prepared for those manipulations, and it helped them prepare for and overcome their susceptibility. This suggested approach is congruent with second responder programs, which use evidence-based, trauma-informed approaches to support victims, divorcing them from the help-seeking and administrative burdens required by traditional service-referral models (Petersen *et al.*, 2022; Rubenstein *et al.*, 2021).

More specifically, victims have shared directly with us that the *five-stage model* could be used to assist other victims in the following:

- Seeing the reality of what will likely happen to them.
- Reducing victim isolation. By sharing the *five-stage model*, victims shared that it would help them to see that these patterns have happened to many other victims.
- Building confidence and regaining control. Abusive relationships are characterized by power and control. By sharing with victims what is likely to happen, victims shared that it would help them build confidence and regain power and control in their relationship trajectory.

Finally, our jail-call study results continue to reinforce that recantation is a by-product of abuser tampering and manipulation. Sometimes the practitioners working with cases in which a victim recants treat the case less seriously, when our results show that abusers' highly sophisticated tampering and manipulation strategies (e.g., sympathy appeals) should prompt a redoubling of professional efforts to hold abusers accountable for their actions.

References

Allison, C.J., K. Bartholomew, O. Mayseless, and D.G. Dutton. 2008. "Love as a battlefield: Dynamics in couples identified for male partner violence." *Journal of Family Issues* 20 (1): 125–150.

Bonomi, A.E., R. Gangamma, C.R. Locke, H. Katafiasz, and D. Martin. 2011. "'Meet me at the hill where we used to park': Interpersonal processes associated with victim recantation." *Social Science and Medicine* 73: 1054–1061.

Bui, H.N. 2001. "Domestic violence victims' behavior in favor of prosecution effects of gender relations." *Women and Criminal Justice* 12 (4): 51–76.

Cala, M., M.E. Trigo, and F.J. Saavedra. 2016. "Women's disengagement from legal proceedings for intimate partner violence: Sociodemographic and psychological variables." *European Journal of Psychology Applied to Legal Context* 8: 35–42.

Camacho, C.M., and L.F. Alarid. 2008. "The significance of the victim advocate for domestic violence victims in municipal court." *Violence and Victims* 23 (3): 288–300.

Dawson, M., and R. Dinovitzer. 2001. "Victim cooperation and the prosecution of domestic violence in a specialized court." *Justice Quarterly* 18 (3): 593–622.

Ellison, L. 2002. "Prosecuting domestic violence without victim participation." *Modern Law Review* 65 (6): 834–858.

Goodman, L., L. Bennett, and M.A. Dutton. 1999. "Obstacles to victims' cooperation with the criminal prosecution of their abusers: The role of social support." *Violence and Victims* 14 (4): 427–444.

Hart, B. 1993. "Battered women and the criminal justice system." *American Behavioral Scientist* 36 (5): 624–638.

Kernic, M., L. Drolette, S. Shanahan, and D. Martin. 2023. *Victim Recantation and Disengagement from Prosecution in Intimate Partner Violence Criminally Prosecuted Crimes in King County.* Washington, DC: Predictors of Victim Recantation and Disengagement and Prosecutorial Outcomes. U.S. Department of Justice, National Institute of Justice (Grant #: 2017-VA-CX-0034).

Pence, E., and M. Paymar. 1993. *Education Groups for Men Who Batter: The Duluth Model.* New York: Springer Publishing Company.

Petersen, K., R.C. Davis, and B.G. Taylor. 2022. "Effects of second responder programs on repeat incidents of family abuse: An updated systematic review and meta-analysis." *Campbell System Review* 18 (1): 1–37.

Roberts, J.C., L. Wolfer, and M. Mele. 2008. "Why victims of intimate partner violence withdraw protection orders." *Journal of Family Violence* 23: 369–375.

Rubenstein, B.Y., M.L.T. Wojcik, V.R. Anderson, and B.S. Fisher. 2021. "Shifting the service referral paradigm using community-based second responders: Examining weapon use in intimate partner violence." *Journal of Family Violence* 36: 527–535.

Interlude to Case Exemplars

In Chapters 1 to 3, we laid the groundwork for case examples (Chapters 4 to 8) to further illustrate abuser tampering to influence recantation: what abusers say, how they say it, and how victims respond. The case examples in Chapters 4 to 8 further detail the *five-stage model*. Chapters 4 to 8 take the reader and listener into a more in-depth discovery of the abuse scene, how the *five-stage model* played out in the jail calls, and the aftermath of recantation. In addition, they extend the *five-stage model's* implications by showing how abusers triangulated third parties—friends and children—into the abuse dynamic (Chapters 7 and 8). The case examples also illustrate how alternative technology modalities (e.g., text messages) are being used to tamper with victims (e.g., Chapter 6), and how victim advocates are supporting victims in buffering against such tampering (Chapter 7). Each couple we encountered in our work over the years has a profoundly unique and impactful story. The case examples reflect a blend of information from and across couples (with altered details)—an approach commonly used in therapeutic training settings to protect confidentiality and safety.

DOI: 10.4324/9781003348696-4

4 So This Is Where You Think I Need to Be?

The Case of John and Amanda

Amanda called 911 crying and screaming, "He is going to kill me . . . he is going to kill me." John was yelling and breaking glass in the background. The call disconnected, and the dispatcher called Amanda back. Amanda answered and shared that John had beaten her and then fled the scene.

Police arrived and found John standing in an alley behind the couple's apartment. John was calm and said that he had just arrived home, that nothing had happened, and that he had not touched Amanda.

Police talked with Amanda inside the apartment. Amanda was having a hard time breathing and said John was mad that she had not made dinner. Amanda worked as a cocktail waitress, was late leaving work, and had fallen asleep with their infant when she got home. Amanda said she woke to John, who was intoxicated, jumping on her and punching her. John bit Amanda's face, causing her to scream. John attempted to quiet

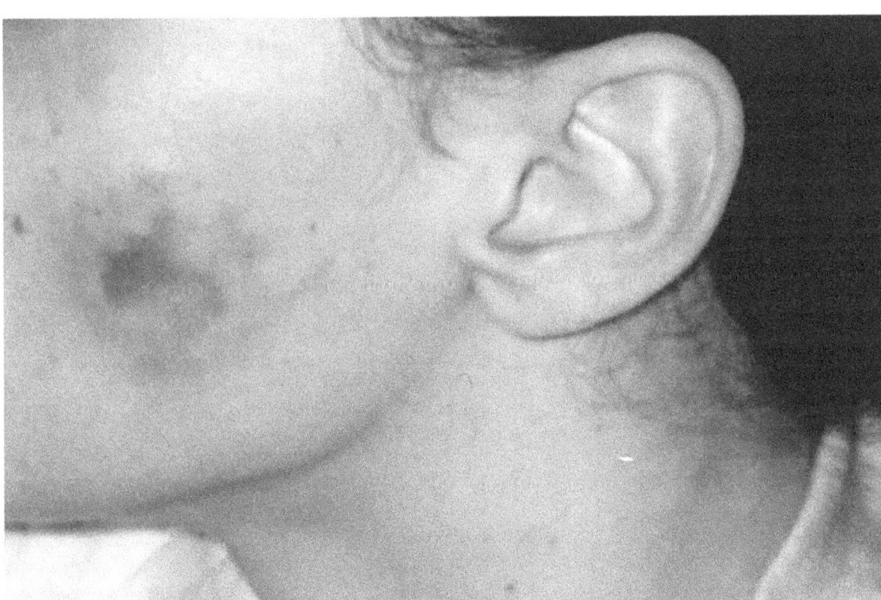

Figure 4.1 John inflicted significant injuries.

DOI: 10.4324/9781003348696-5

Amanda by covering her nose and mouth with a blanket. Amanda said that her vision went black, and she saw stars and flashes of light.

Police took numerous photographs of Amanda's injuries and of the scene. The injuries John inflicted were not minor. Figure 4.1 shows the bruising John inflicted by biting Amanda's face.

In a photo taken of the couple's bedroom, John had pinned pictures of women in hypersexualized poses (Figure 4.2). John's pinups bothered Amanda; she was self-conscious about her weight after giving birth to their infant. Amanda believed John was trying to shame her about her weight gain.

Another photograph taken by the police at the scene shows that John had broken their bedroom door (Figure 4.3).

John was arrested and booked in jail. Within two hours of being booked and still intoxicated, John began calling Amanda from jail. John's calls to Amanda followed the patterns in the *five-stage model* with one exception: John used veiled threats to influence Amanda's intention to recant. John threatened Amanda saying that pressing charges would be the "worst mistake" Amanda had ever made. When Amanda confronted John

Figure 4.2 John pinned pictures of women in hypersexualized poses on their bedroom wall.

Figure 4.3 John broke their bedroom door.

that him saying "worst mistake" sounded like a threat, John told her he meant he would end the relationship with her, and she would be without someone who loved her. He knew this was an outcome that Amanda did not want; Amanda had been estranged from her family of origin for years.

Amanda recanted. In the days following Amanda's 911 call, and after multiple calls from John, Amanda minimized the abuse. In Amanda's interview with a detective, she tried to hide John's bite marks with makeup. She denied that John had punched, bitten, and suffocated her. Amanda appeared at John's bail hearing and told the judge that John was a good partner and father and that John had "too much to drink and needed anger management classes" because he grew up in an abusive home. Amanda asked for the no-contact order to be removed and bail lowered. The judge denied Amanda's request. Amanda then posted bail for John.

After charges were filed, the jail calls between John and Amanda occurred and were later discovered by prosecutors. John accepted a guilty plea to increased charges instead of a jury trial. John was sentenced for felony domestic violence assault, witness tampering, and violations of a no-contact order.

The event that led to Amanda calling 911 was the first interaction that Amanda had with the police regarding John's abuse.

Those interested in eliminating domestic violence ask the following: What did John say to Amanda when he called her from jail to influence her to recant? How was he saying it? How did Amanda respond?

Stage 1: Arguing About and Minimizing the Abuse

In the first call that John made to Amanda, emotions were high. Only two hours had passed since John was booked into jail. John and Amanda argued about what happened.

John accused Amanda of putting him in jail: "So this is where you think I need to be right [in jail]? All this because you wanna act stupid . . . you're a fuckin' snitch-ass bitch."

John blamed Amanda for being late, baselessly accusing her of having an affair with one of her customers. Amanda's response was sarcastic: "Yaaaah. That's what I was doin' ", which was evidence of her agency and self-determination in resisting John's accusations. The conversation continued.

John: Over some trick. You were half hour late over some trick.
Amanda: Because, uh, his credit card was not going through. It was declining and shit. He owed me a hundred bucks.
(long pause)
Amanda: For sucking his dick, right?
John: Is that what you were doin'?
Amanda: (sighs) Yaaaah. That's what I was doin'.
John: I mean, I bet. Probably.

Amanda continued to exercise agency in their early conversations by telling John that she was afraid he was going to kill her. John continued to blame Amanda for the abuse.

Amanda: You were gonna kill me! This is the second time I've felt like I, I almost died. You covered my mouth and my fuckin' nose and I feel like I'm gonna fuckin' die . . . I can't breathe. You were, like, smothering me to death.
John: You never try to say sorry and apologize to me. You know I've got a bad temper. You add fuel to the fire by saying weird shit to me, saying "you'll never see your son again" and stuff like that.

Stage 2: Appealing to the Victim's Sympathy

After arguing over what happened during the abuse event, John appealed to Amanda's sympathy by reminding her how much he was suffering in jail: "So you're goin' to try to hit me with a felony here, right . . . you're not in here [jail] . . . I am!" This positioned John as the "victim," and Amanda responded with empathy and concern for John's well-being: "And you don't think I've slept knowing my baby's dad is in jail right now? I want that baby to see your face every day."

As noted in Chapter 2, the *five-stage model* did not unfold linearly; couples often cycled through stages multiple times. In this regard, just days away from appearing in court, John continued to appeal to Amanda's sympathy. John reminded Amanda of his workplace stressors, how he felt about the long hours he was away from his family, and his troubles with alcohol.

Stage 3: Connecting Over Common Ground

John and Amanda also connected over common ground. John conveyed that he loved Amanda so deeply that he could not bear the thought that he punched her for not having dinner on the table. John thought it was sexy that Amanda was a cocktail waitress, but he was also jealous that she interacted with other men. John insisted that he loved Amanda.

John brought up that he wanted to spend more time with Amanda and their infant. This was triggered by his fears that Amanda would leave him. Amanda told John that police warned her to leave John before he killed her.

In response to John's overtures of love and care, Amanda minimized her injuries saying, e.g., "I never bled at all." Wanting a connection with John, Amanda asked, "Don't you want to see your son?" John affirmed that he did and allowed Amanda to visit him in jail.

Stages 4 and 5: Recantation Request and Instructions

Abusers in our jail-call analysis manipulated victims and directly requested that they recant (Bonomi *et al.*, 2011). John did the same, reinforced with a veiled threat. John told Amanda that if she "went against him, it's gonna be the worst mistake you've ever done in your whole life. I guarantee you."

Amanda cautioned John about threatening her when their call was being recorded. John then softened his tone and clarified that "the worst mistake" meant he would leave Amanda.

John's threat to end the relationship instilled fear in Amanda (she wanted to remain intimately connected to John) and strengthened their connection. Even though Amanda believed John deserved to be in jail, Amanda took the lead on strategizing what to say in court so that she and John could be reunited. Like other couples in our jail-call study, the process of "reuniting" often involved conjuring ideas of earlier, happier times (*Stage 3*). The title of our study "*Meet Me at the Hill Where We Used to Park*" was a direct quote used by an abuser when reminiscing about the "hill" where they used to "park" and have sex (Bonomi *et al.*, 2011).

Throughout John and Amanda's conversations, Amanda offered the idea that John was an abuser because he grew up seeing his parents fight, he had been under the influence of alcohol, and he did not know what he was doing. John resisted Amanda's ideas. However,

Amanda's constant refrain was that John needed help. Following, Amanda instructed John to tell the judge he was in a "blackout" and needs "anger management" classes.

John: I will see what the judge has to say and I'm gonna say what I have to say but pretty much I'm, I'm going to stick with my story . . . I, I didn't even touch you.
Amanda: I wouldn't do that because then you're lying . . . be up front, be like "I was out of control drunk, I was in a blackout. I would normally, I would've never done something like that."
John: And that I, I need anger management, I need to start going to classes, I need to request days off to go to anger management? NO!
Amanda: But you need to tell the judge that you do need that.
John: I don't need it.
Amanda: So that they'll let you the fuck out of there, otherwise they're going to keep you in there.

Amanda exercised *her* agency in helping to establish the plan for what they would say in court. However, as we observed in the jail-call study (Bonomi *et al.*, 2011), it was *the couple's* agency that ultimately prevailed through their common purpose, uniting "against the court" to help John get out of jail.

Summary

Even though Amanda believed John deserved to be in jail, John's tampering and manipulation were effective in influencing Amanda to recant her story. After many calls and manipulations, Amanda said John was the person she wanted to be with. When strategizing about what to say in court, Amanda instructed John to tell the judge that he was in a "blackout" and needed "anger management" classes. John attended many anger management classes over the years, but he did not stop abusing Amanda. John strangled, punched, kicked, burned, raped, and degraded Amanda. After many years, through professional support and moving to a confidential domestic violence shelter, Amanda left John to escape the violence and start a new life. This case illustrates what many victims have shared with us during our presentations of the *five-stage model*: the emotional manipulation used by their abuser is "so deep" and "powerful" and even though victims know the manipulation is happening, it may take them years to identify how it is happening and impacting them. This was the case with Amanda, who endured abuse for years before separating from John through the help of professionals.

Reference

Bonomi, A.E., R. Gangamma, C.R. Locke, H. Katafiasz, and D. Martin. 2011. "'Meet me at the hill where we used to park': Interpersonal processes associated with victim recantation." *Social Science and Medicine* 73: 1054–1061.

5 If I Lost You, It's Like Losing an Arm or Something

The Case of Jake and Charlene

Jake arrived high and drunk at Charlene's apartment and found her asleep on the couch. Jake shook Charlene awake to ask if she wanted a hamburger. Charlene said she didn't. Charlene was a vegetarian—one of Charlene's "behaviors" that "bothered" Jake. Jake screamed, "Why are you always acting like you're better than me?!"

Jake kicked open the door to leave the apartment. Charlene yelled after Jake, "Fine just leave [me] and go fuck your girlfriend!" Jake had slept with several women over the last year, and he and Charlene regularly "argued" about this. These "arguments" involved Jake beating Charlene.

Jake stormed back into the apartment and pinned Charlene down on the couch. Jake spit in Charlene's face. He repeatedly punched Charlene and broke her wrist. Jake put his hands around Charlene's neck and strangled her, until she saw stars.

Charlene screamed that Jake would face consequences: "You already have a record of doing these things to other women!" Jake had prior criminal domestic violence convictions.

Charlene was weak from being strangled and could not get to the phone to call for help. However, neighbors heard Charlene screaming and called 911.

When the police arrived at the scene, they chased down Jake and arrested him. Police took photos of bruising to Charlene's neck from strangulation (Figure 5.1).

Jake was booked into jail and immediately called Charlene. In the calls between Jake and Charlene, the patterns observed in the *five-stage model* unfolded. Jake sounded like a sophisticated manipulator. In a single sentence, Jake would interchange professed love, care, and concern for Charlene (*Stage 3*) with blaming her for the abuse (*Stage 1*). Jake claimed to be a "visionary," sharing a dream he had of Charlene contracting a major illness to try to instill fear in her. Jake described seeing himself as unique, a loner, and with underlying mental health vulnerabilities, which he used to manipulate Charlene into feeling sorry for him (*Stage 2*). Jake and Charlene were both musicians and described feeling that the love they shared was different and could not be understood by others (*Stage 3*), including the criminal justice system (*Stages 4 and 5*). Conversations that centered on books and music solidified their bond and connection to each other.

Here are how the conversations went.

Stage 1: Arguing About and Minimizing the Abuse

In their early conversations, Jake and Charlene argued about the abuse. Jake pressed Charlene about whether she told police that he was going to kill her. Did you tell police

DOI: 10.4324/9781003348696-6

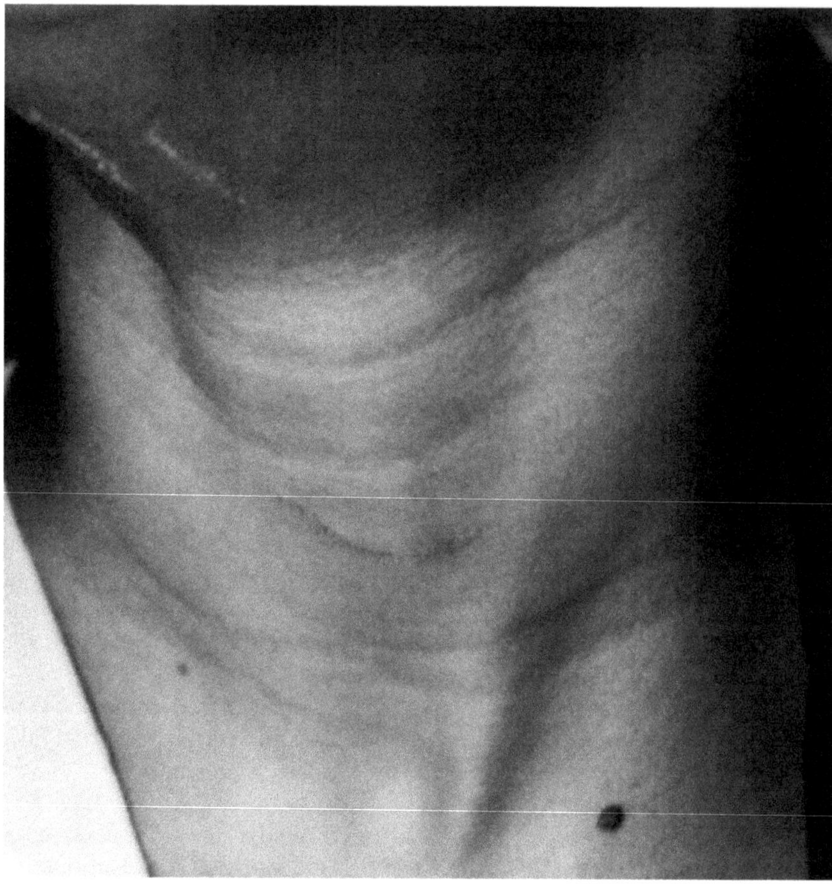

Figure 5.1 Bruising from strangulation.

"that I was going to kill you?" Charlene denied telling police that Jake was going to kill her. However, Charlene told a victim advocate: "Jake could have killed me that night, it was that serious."

Charlene's agency and determination to hold Jake accountable were strong. Charlene confronted Jake about beating her. In response, Jake deflected responsibility and claimed he was the "victim" of Charlene's verbal abuse.

Charlene: Why are you constantly beating on me, though?
Jake: I'm not constantly beating on you . . . you, you don't understand that you beat on me with words and I can't defend myself.
Charlene: With words, but I don't hit you.
Jake: Hit me, you hit me so fuckin' hard mentally, I'm a very fragile person . . . mentally.
Charlene: I would, I would rather um be verbally attacked.
Jake: I would never want to be verbally attacked in my state, it's always a defense and then me taking it to the point where you get my level going over the flip-side and I lose it like the Incredible Hulk.

Jake continued to deflect responsibility and blame Charlene for what he saw as her causing him to be abusive: "You have a way of, of fucking someone's head up, er, that's what really made me snap, when you said, 'go fuck [your ex-girlfriend], go fuck [your ex-girlfriend], go back to your [ex-girlfriend].' "

Stage 2: Appealing to Her Sympathy

In addition to blaming Charlene, Jake played the "victim" by appealing to Charlene's sympathy. Jake used analogies and metaphors from books he was reading (in jail) to describe how different and alone he felt, and to conjure Charlene's care and concern for him.

Jake described that he identified with Martin Pistorius in his personal memoir *Ghost Boy* (Pistorius, 2011). Pistorius at the age of 12 years fell sick, became mute and wheelchair bound, and suffered social isolation. Jake used the image of Pistorius to allude to his own vulnerabilities in jail—Jake described how he was different from others in jail, a loner, keeping to himself.

In addition, Jake skillfully wove together discussions of *Ghost Boy*, the Bible, and "relationship books," which reinforced his commitment to rehabilitate from the abuse he inflicted on Charlene. For example, Jake told Charlene that he was reading books on relationships and how to "get it right and everything, what I need to do to get myself together." Jake tried to reassure Charlene: "Don't worry about us, I worry about me and you worry about you and we get ourselves together and we'll come together and we won't have no worries. OK?"

Jake also appealed to Charlene's sympathy by saying he wished he could go back in time to change his actions. Jake said that instead of beating Charlene, he wished he could have hugged her. However, Jake positioned himself as the "victim" by describing his fear that Charlene would have rejected his hug:

> I just keep seeing that day over and over again, like I wish I would have reached out and hugged you . . . but I was fearful that you would have rejected me, I was fearful because you've done it so many times. I was fearful.

While Jake felt vulnerable that Charlene would reject his hug, Charlene exercised concern and her agency by calling Jake out on his bad behavior: "I don't know where your fear and anger and guilt and all of this stuff comes from, but I know it's not all me."

Stage 3: Connecting Over Common Ground

Jake and Charlene were both musicians and felt the love they shared was "different" and could not be understood by others, including the criminal justice system. Conversations that centered on books and music solidified their bond and connection to each other.

During one jail call, Charlene played "their song"—the Dave Matthews Band's *Stay or Leave* (2003; some song lyrics are reproduced in the following conversation). The haunting refrain of the song (see lyrics that read, "*Stay or leave/I want you not to go/But you did*") served to activate their shared connection and their fears of losing each other if Jake remained in jail. Their conversation went as follows.

Charlene: Do you want to hear the song you like or the other song?
Jake: Our song.

[Song starts to play.]
Stay or leave
I want you not to go
But you should
It was good, as good goes
Stay or leave
I want you not to go
But you did.

Jake: [Sighing, sniffling, crying] There is our song. . . . It's like opening or something. Expressing. It's sad but beautiful.

Charlene: It makes me cry, too.

Jake: It reminds me of our times at the spa too.

Charlene: It's sort of a beautiful thing, but it's like I could feel your spirit moving with the song.

The purpose of Charlene playing the song was to unite Jake and Charlene over shared memories (e.g., their time at a spa) and a spiritual connection. Charlene said she could feel Jake's spirit moving with the song. After bonding over their song, Jake then professed that if he lost Charlene, "it would be like losing an arm or something," which served both as a sympathy appeal (*Stage 3*) and a pursuit of Charlene's love and their shared connection.

Charlene described her love for Jake as having a spell cast on her:

> Like you're, you're my friend, and you're, you're my lover, you're my everything, I mean, you know . . . I've tried to tell myself that it's over but I just can't do it. . . . I dunno what's wrong with me. I feel like somebody cast a spell on me or something, cause I used to be a lot stronger mentally, be able to just walk away, but I can't.

Even though Charlene reported feeling that she was under Jake's "love spell," she also expressed agency and set boundaries with Jake about what she wanted and needed from him. Jake responded by suggesting he would "put a ring on her finger" (marry her). The recording of their conversation was as follows.

Charlene: I'm just going to tell you, I'm just going to let you know this.

Jake: (softly) mmm, hmmm.

Charlene: That from this point on and from the point after, whenever, whenever things are uh come to their resolve as far as the legal, the legalities of it all—

Jake: (softly) Yes.

Charlene: I, I'm just letting you know that if you want, I, I, I'm going to refrain myself and I'm going to continue on with my life, but when, if you truly ever loved me and if you still love me when you, when you leave [pause] and you really want to have a relationship with someone, I don't mean just say I love you and just drop in—

Jake: (softly) Yes.

Charlene: . . . and out, but I mean it, I mean it—

Jake: (softly) Yes, put a ring on your finger—

Charlene: I mean it, if you truly want a wife—

Jake: (softly) Yes.
Charlene: . . . a woman, someone to love and care about you.
Jake: Yah.

Charlene said more about what she wanted out of the relationship with Jake:

> There may be children and there may not be. . . . I may have my own and I-they may be adopted or somebody else's but I'm gonna have a house . . . and a life . . . just want to be happy, mature and handle my life, and live a life, possibly write a book, and ya know, and, just be happy . . . I'm going to have a responsible, uh, marriage, and I'm going to be happy and I'm goin' to do things that are productive and that are nice and I'm gonna have—I just envision a very pleasant rest of my life . . . Ya know, I don't want to be alone.

Charlene also shared her vulnerabilities and strengths:

> I don't accept kindness very well because somewhere in myself I feel I don't deserve it because of what I've been through in life. But I know I'm a good person and I have a lot of talent . . . but I need to get—find a center so that I can be at peace and happy with or without somebody . . . It's not all about uh fame or glories or anything . . . it's just about loving myself and loving the person that loves me and, and doing the right thing, basically. And, ya know, that's karma.

Stages 4 and 5: Asking Her to Recant, Giving Instructions

Jake and Charlene discussed recantation throughout their conversations. But Jake's direct request for Charlene to recant and instructions occurred late in the conversations.

Jake: If you would, would let them know what you feel about me, that you're not scared of me and you know, that we will further our relationship after my rehabilitation and plans and stuff like that, you know . . . I love you, more than all of this and you know, this is just one part of our lives and we have something that's everlasting and this is not the whole of it or the amount to a great deal. This is not how I see you and this is not how you see me . . . I'm thankful that you're strong and focus first spiritually . . . to be true to yourself and me.
Charlene: Well, there's nobody like you, so.

Charlene indicated she "even wrote a letter to the judge, telling them that, 'I don't want a no-contact order, that I think you need to get um-other help besides um, you know, jail and stuff, I told them that, I don't—that's not what I wanted.'" Charlene apologized and reassured Jake that she was still committed to him: "I still love you too and I'm sorry, you know, I'm sorry, I-I don't know what else to say . . . nothing's changed, you know, I'm not seeing anybody, er."

To further manipulate Charlene, Jake described how he was getting good at reading dreams. Jake described a dream he had about Charlene being sick and hospitalized from smoking cigarettes.

As Charlene and Jake navigated conversations about recantation, Charlene instructed Jake on what he could/should say to the judge.

Charlene: I would plead guilty . . . and I would admit that I have been intoxicated . . . you don't have to name the exact substance but I would make that of issue because I brought it up.
Jake: That, that.
Charlene: And, I think, if you, if you admit to it.
Jake: That I was intoxicated?
Charlene: Yah. I think if you admit to, if you admit to, they will probably give you, uh, a different kind of sentencing, you, you won't have to be in jail, you will get therapy, you will get other resources.
Jake: Was I, was I intoxicated?
Charlene: Well, I, I believe you were.

As Jake and Charlene worked on recantation plans, they continued to bond over their shared connection, with Charlene noting she got her "eyebrows pierced" and Jake responding with "Well, my goatee grew back . . . my fingernails are long and I'm not cutting them till I touch you . . . I'll let you cut em, okay?"

Summary and Aftermath

Even though Charlene held Jake accountable for his abuse, Jake's tampering and manipulations worked to erode Charlene's agency and influence her recantation. Jake manipulated Charlene by describing his mental health vulnerabilities and blamed Charlene for instigating his abuse. Jake and Charlene bonded over the special love they shared, which they felt could not be understood by others. Conversations that revolved around books and music solidified their bond and connection to each other.

After Charlene recanted and after Jake entered a plea, Jake called Charlene again. Jake wanted to know if it was possible for them to have a relationship again when he got out of custody. While Charlene loved and cared for Jake, Charlene ended the conversation and reported feeling confused and scared. Charlene called a victim advocate after talking with Jake, which led to additional sanction for Jake violating a no-contact order.

At sentencing for Jake's (additional) abuse, Charlene provided the following victim impact statement to the court:

> To begin, I now have come to know that I had been manipulated, taken advantage of, and abused on many levels. . . . I have also lost money, and time- caring for him, of who has never maintained any job, substantial income, and has never maintained a residence in a whole of about five years I have known of him and had intimate relations. I felt ashamed for taking the terrible abuse, did not call the police, cried, and swore it was over. I felt helpless and tired, and it was hard enough to try to maintain and better my own situation. I am a strong person, being, and character and no man has ever abused me physically or manipulated me as he has done. Neither have I ever expected to be in such a situation of abuse. I will say he has a lot of charm, although misplaced. This whole nightmare of a situation is truly beyond any of my common understanding. I have lost two of the only family and loved ones all in one year, as well as my job and home at one point also I believe due to his carelessness and

> possessiveness. I do thank the justice system, for every time. And I believe somewhat of justice has prevailed, although it will never repay the truth and ultimate pain as well as soul depravation this sorry excuse for a man has taken and done to me and from my life.

Charlene's victim impact statement illustrates what many victims have shared with us during our presentations of the *five-stage model*: that the emotional manipulation used by their abuser is "so deep"—and even though victims know the emotional abuse is happening—the manipulation is "so powerful" that it may take time to understand the full extent of how it is happening and impacting them.

After Jake was released from prison, he started a new relationship with another woman—Brenda. Shortly into the relationship, Jake threatened to kill Brenda for sleeping with another man. Jake tracked down Brenda, beat her, and strangled her. Brenda called the police, and Jake was arrested and soon after returned to prison.

References

Matthews, D. 2003. "Stay (wasting time)." *The Central Park Concert*. RCA Records.

Pistorius, M. 2011. *Ghost Boy*. New York: Simon and Schuster.

6 She Needs to Show Up Tomorrow and Say She Was Lying

The Case of Shawn and Tasha

When police first saw Tasha, she was barefoot in a video store parking lot at four o'clock in the morning. The left side of her face was bruised; her eye was swollen shut. Tasha was crying, scared for her life. Her boyfriend Shawn had just beaten and strangled her.

When police arrived, Tasha told them what happened. She described a "normal evening gone violently wrong." Shawn had come home late and became upset when Tasha tried to let the dog outside. Shawn slapped Tasha, telling her not to argue, ordering her to "be nice."

Shawn then threw Tasha to the floor, pinned her down, and strangled her saying "I'm going to make you see stars." Shawn pressed his thumbs into Tasha's eyes and punched her in the face.

Tasha tried to leave the apartment, but Shawn pushed and kicked her away from the door, locking it with a key. Given their history, Tasha knew Shawn would not let her go. Shawn put his arm around Tasha and asked, "[W]hy do you have to act like that?" He even promised to unlock the door so Tasha could leave "freely."

Shawn packed his things to leave but felt bad when he saw that Tasha's eye started to swell. So, Shawn stopped and got some ice for Tasha.

Shawn told Tasha that he was sorry. He wanted to have sex. Tasha told him, "No. I don't want to do this." Shawn tore off Tasha's pants and underwear despite her protests. Shawn pinned Tasha down and penetrated her, telling her, "It will be okay." Tasha continued to say "no."

After Shawn raped Tasha, Shawn fell asleep. Tasha later reported feeling afraid for her life. A barefoot and battered Tasha fled the apartment and called the police.

The police and ambulance arrived. Police found Shawn asleep. Shawn told police Tasha attacked him with a knife, used drugs, and tried to take his life by suicide. Shawn claimed he was "defending himself." Despite Shawn's pleas, police arrested him for physical assault and took him to jail.

Tasha went to the hospital in an ambulance. She was angry and hurt. She received care for her injuries. Tasha was asked at the hospital if she had ever "been forced by someone to have sex when you did not want it." Tasha said yes.

The Phone Calls Start and Cycle Through All Five Stages, Repeatedly

Shawn and Tasha's interactions provide an example of the continuous flow through the *five-stage model*, with Tasha's agency (i.e., self-determination) ebbing and flowing in response to Shawn's tampering.

DOI: 10.4324/9781003348696-7

In the first example, Shawn called Tasha soon after being arrested and booked into jail to say he was sorry, that he missed her and loved her (*Stage 3*). Tasha did not forgive Shawn (*Stage 1*), but as she hung up the phone, her face still swollen and her neck still sore, she was willing to talk to him again.

Shawn continued to call Tasha from jail dozens of times. Shawn's tampering with Tasha was sophisticated and relentless.

Shawn used a "soft approach," professing to Tasha his contrition, personal growth, and change (*Stage 3*). Shawn repeated his promise that he had changed, that he loved her, and that it was drugs and mental health that caused him to be violent (*Stage 2*). He called Tasha his "wife" to encourage her closeness (*Stage 3*) and prime her to recant (*Stage 4*).

Shawn: Are we still gonna get married?
Tasha: No.
Shawn: Hmm.
Tasha: No.
Shawn: What?
Tasha: Then you, you're going to kill me.
Shawn: No, I'm not.
Tasha: Yeah, you will. There's nothing left. Fucking blackened both my eyes multiple times. Fucking broke my head. Fucked up my shoulder. Fucked my neck up. Fucked my throat up. Fucked up my head. Put a plate through my head. Cause I, you saw that wiped ketchup on you when I didn't.
Shawn: I am sorry baby. It's just that.

For example, in one conversation Shawn elicited a positive reaction from Tasha when he pleaded that he missed her (*Stage 2*). However, Tasha then resisted Shawn's sympathy appeal by detailing the abuse she suffered (*Stage 1*),

Tasha: I don't fucking want shit to do with you.
Shawn: You don't miss me at all?
Tasha: What would I miss? The getting my ass kicked, being bruised every day. Having to make up a different fucking lie to, for the bruises on my arms and the bruises on my face. Or do I miss you spitting on me? Or do I miss you kicking me? Or do I miss my shoulder dislocating every time I fucking try to wash my hair and shit? Cuz he fucking threw me by my arm. Do I? Is that what I missed? Is that what you're talking about?
Shawn: Look, I'm, that wasn't, that wasn't right.
Tasha: Or do I or do I miss seeing my fucking, the inside of my car? My airbags fucked up every day cuz you fucking threw a temper tantrum and and hit it.
Shawn: I'm telling you that I've changed.

Tasha's tone describing Shawn's abuse sounded strong and was detailed; her agency was resurgent. Hearing Tasha's account provides an understanding of the breadth of what she went through, and how, even now with Shawn's apologies, his abuse was too much to forgive or forget (*Stage 1*). Each time, Shawn apologized for his abuse and said he wouldn't do it again. Tasha believed him, her agency and resistance diminishing.

However, over time, Shawn's sympathy appeals became less convincing; Tasha's agency resurged.

Tasha: No, it's because like how, come when you made me come back in the house. You knew you were gonna be mean. Did you?
Shawn: No baby. I don't, I don't ever plan it. Like, I always like, I'm always cool and then it's just like the factors. It's like I was just tired and it's—
Tasha: Like, then how come as soon as you shut the door. It happened. Like as soon as I came back in the house, you shut the door.
Shawn: Oh, because remember I even unlocked it. So you feel safe. I just like—
Tasha: Here. Yeah. But then you in that same, in that same spot. We didn't even move anywhere in that same spot. You pushed me down and remember you were on me. He was going, you were gonna see stars, you're gonna see stars, you're gonna see stars.
Shawn: I am so sorry baby.
Tasha: I don't wanna see stars.

Shawn and Tasha's interactions are an example of the continuous flow through the *five-stage model*, with Tasha's agency ebbing and flowing in response to Shawn's tampering with her. Figure 6.1 represents how this played out.

In a second example of the *five-stage model* playing out continuously, Shawn downplayed his abuse saying he was drunk (*Stage 1*) and was "going through some shit" including mental health issues (*Stage 2*). Shawn then tearfully apologized and told Tasha he loved her and that she was his "wife," even though they weren't married (*Stage 3*).

Shortly after this phone call, Shawn called Tasha and was unable to reach her. He therefore left her a voice message saying that he missed her (*Stage 3*) and instructed her on what to say to the prosecutor (*Stages 4 and 5*):

> Hey baby boo. I miss you big time. I went to court today you know. It's not looking good so far. I don't know we should get through this. All you have to do is just

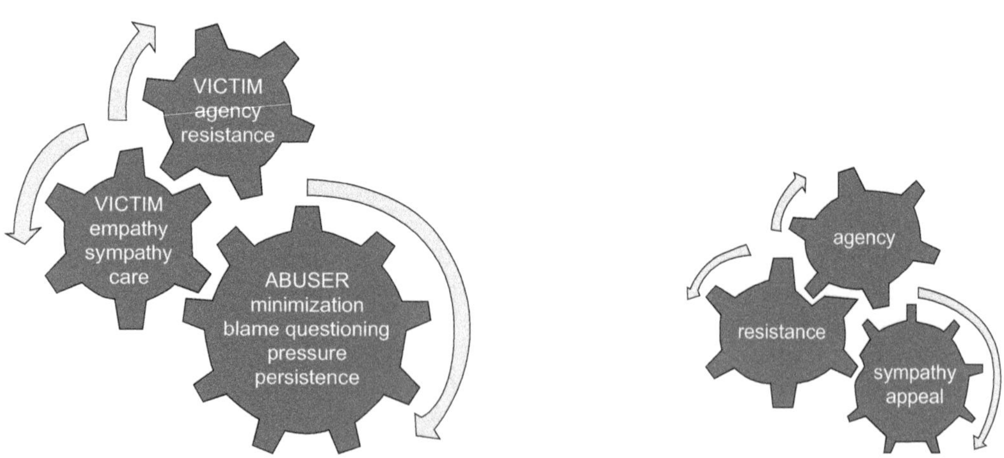

Figure 6.1 Continuous flow through the *five-stage model*, with victim agency ebbing and flowing.

give the prosecutor a call and just tell him that nothing happened. And that number is 296–9000. I don't know baby I'll see you soon. I love you. . . . Bye (*kisses over phone*). . .. Alright baby."

Shawn's Use of Third Parties to Tamper With Tasha

Shawn's calls to Tasha were in violation of a court-issued no-contact order to protect Tasha. As such, Shawn's calls to Tasha were prevented from going through, as they were placed under a jail-imposed "administrative phone block."

Shawn found a way around the administrative block to Tasha's number. Shawn used three-way connections to tamper with and wear down Tasha. The jail phone system is designed to prevent three-way calls. If the system detects an attempt at a three-way call, it disconnects the call. However, to disguise the sound of the three-way function, Shawn blew into the phone to circumvent the system.

Shawn called his friends and family to plot ways to convince Tasha to recant and refuse prosecution efforts. For example, Shawn called his mother and asked, "Can you like offer her some money to get her to drop it?"

In another example, Shawn tried to convince his friend Jerry to pressure Tasha to "retract" her statement and in turn Shawn would protect Jerry from any harm.

Shawn: Dog I, its, dog its hella important that I talk to her dog. Can you hear me?

Jerry (friend): Yeah. You want me to pass her that number or what do you want me tell her?

Shawn: Dog I want you to show up to her fucking work man. And beat that bitch in her fucking face, in her fucking rat. Jesus Christ dog. Dog give her that fucking number dog and tell her to fucking sit the fuck down and shut up. Can you do that?

The conversation concluded with Shawn reminding Jerry of the main purpose of their efforts: to prevent Tasha from showing up in court: "If it she doesn't show up, it all goes away." Jerry said he would talk to Tasha and noted how sad and frightened Tasha seems to be. Jerry told Shawn he was going to "infiltrate."

In his calls to friends and family, Shawn was cruel, violent, and remorseless. Shawn could not refer to Tasha without calling her names such as "the bitch," "the idiot," and "the snitch." Shawn also called Tasha these names directly, as did many of the abusers reflected in our study (Bonomi *et al.*, 2011).

Summary

Shawn and Tasha's interactions exemplify the continuous flow through the *five-stage model*, with Tasha's agency (i.e., self-determination) ebbing and flowing. In some instances, Tasha's agency seemed strong (e.g., calling Shawn out on his bad behavior: "[W]hat would I miss. . . getting my ass kicked, being bruised every day"). In other instances, Shawn's tactics wore down Tasha's agency. When Shawn could not successfully reach Tasha on the phone, he left voice messages conveying terms of endearment and love—for example, "Hey baby boo. I miss you big time"—interspersed with instructions to assist him in getting out of jail: "All you have to do is just give the prosecutor a call and just tell him that nothing happened."

This case example also shows how Shawn involved third parties such as family and friends during jail calls to further tamper with and wear down Tasha.

Tasha continued the relationship with Shawn for several years until his threats to kill her overwhelmed her, and she sought refuge at a friend's house in Canada.

Reference

Bonomi, A.E., R. Gangamma, C.R. Locke, H. Katafiasz, and D. Martin. 2011. "'Meet me at the hill where we used to park': Interpersonal processes associated with victim recantation." *Social Science and Medicine* 73: 1054–1061.

7 Feed and Nurture the "Good Wolf"

The Case of Vincent and Tracy

Vincent dated Tracy from freshman year of high school to Tracy's second year in dental hygiene school. During the relationship, Vincent was angry and jealous. Throughout their relationship, Vincent frequently threatened to harm Tracy and her loved ones. "Choices" was a word that Vincent used to signal to Tracy that she "had a role" in the abuse he would inflict.

Vincent's abuse was so severe that Tracy kept an electronic file of everything he did and often complied with his many demands. Vincent accused Tracy of cheating on him, checked her activities (whom she would see, where she would go), and made Tracy send him pictures to prove she was not with another man. In one example, Vincent demanded that Tracy send a trio of cellphone photos timed precisely five minutes apart, whereby Tracy could "prove" she was not with another man. In those cellphone photos, Vincent demanded that Tracy alter her hairstyle in each picture to "prove" she was not "photoshopping the images."

Early on, Tracy complied. Tracy cared for Vincent and believed in his promises of love and a future together. Tracy wrote letters to say she hoped Vincent would heed the story of the two wolves (Figure 7.1). The story of the two wolves comes from a Cherokee elder teaching his grandson about life (Two Wolves: A Cherokee Legend [https://www.firstpeople.us/FP-Html-Legends/TwoWolves-Cherokee.html]). The elder describes:

> A fight is going on inside me . . . it is a terrible fight and it is between two wolves. One is evil—he is anger, envy, sorrow, regret, greed, arrogance, self-pity, guilt, resentment, inferiority, lies, false pride, superiority, and ego. . . . The other [wolf] is good—he is joy, peace, love, hope, serenity, humility, kindness, benevolence, empathy, generosity, truth, compassion, and faith. The same fight is going on inside you—and inside every other person, too . . . [the wolf that wins is] "The one you feed."

Tracy wrote that she hoped Vincent would feed and nurture the "good wolf" inside him and get professional help.

However, while Tracy loved and cared for Vincent, over time she began to push back on his abuse. And that's when Vincent's abuse escalated.

Vincent sent a text message to Tracy that if she did not marry him, he would punish her by killing her parents (Figure 7.2).

Tracy did not report Vincent's abuse to police. However, Tracy was concerned about her safety and the safety of her family members. Thus, Tracy shared Vincent's threatening

DOI: 10.4324/9781003348696-8

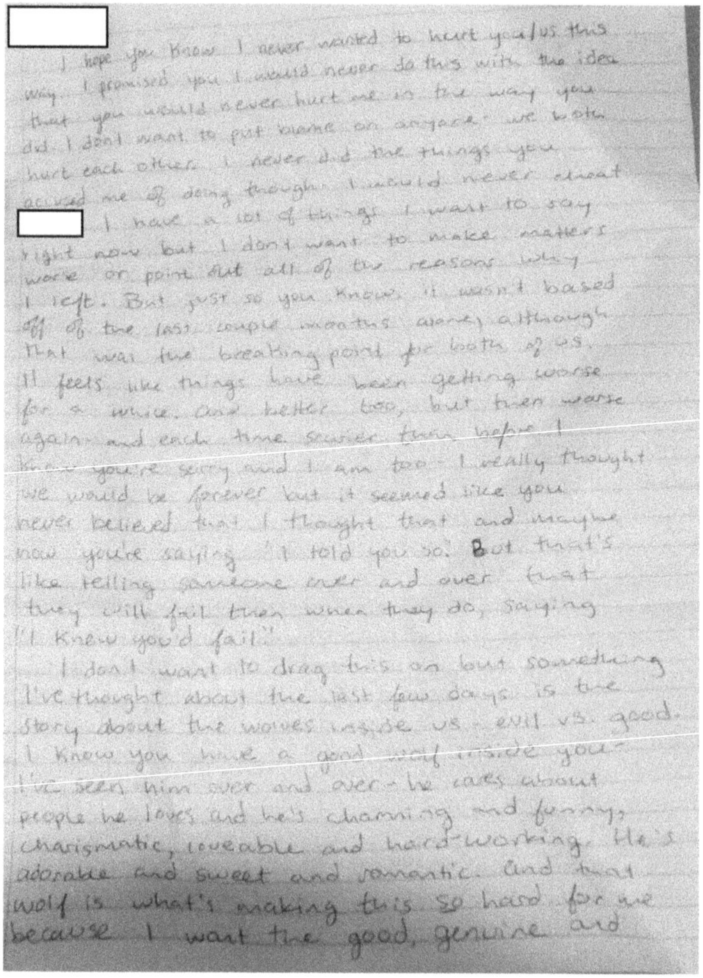

I hope you know I never wanted to hurt you/us this way. I promised you I would never do this with the idea that you would never hurt me in the way you did. I don't want to put blame on anyone – we both hurt each other. I never did the things you accused me of doing though. I would never cheat.

I have a lot of things I want to say right now but I don't want to make matters worse or point out all of the reasons why I left. But just so you know, it wasn't based off of the last couple months alone, although that was the breaking point for both of us. It feels like things have been getting worse for a while. And better too, but then worse again and each time scarier than before. I know you're sorry and I am too. I really thought we would be forever but it seemed like you never believed that I thought that and maybe now you're saying "I told you so." But that's like telling someone over and over that they will fail then when they do, saying "I knew you'd fail."

I don't want to drag this on but something I've thought about the last few days is the story about the wolves inside us – evil vs. good. I know you have a good wolf inside you – I've seen him over and over – he cares about people he loves and he's charming and funny, charismatic, loveable and hard-working. He's adorable and sweet and romantic. And that wolf is what's making this so hard for me because I want the good, genuine and

Figure 7.1 Tracy's letter to Vincent, intentionally redacted to protect Tracy's identity.

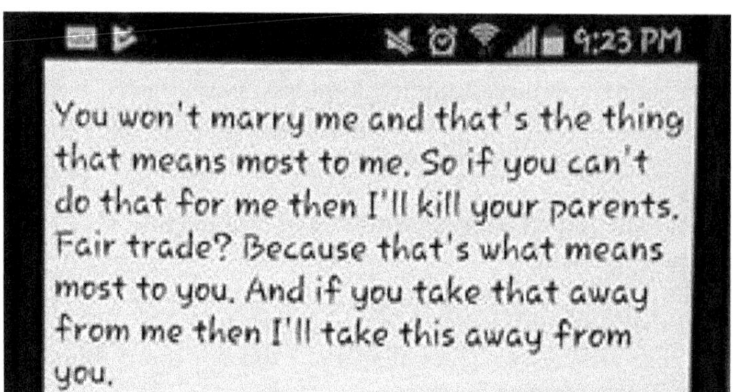

Figure 7.2 Vincent threatens to kill Tracy's parents.

text messages. Family members contacted police, and Vincent was charged with domestic violence crimes.

While Vincent was in jail pending trial, he called Tracy. Vincent said he would take his life by suicide—especially if Tracy were to cheat on him while awaiting trial and sentencing (*Stage 2*).

During one call, Vincent and Tracy connected over their care and longing for each other (*Stage 3*). Vincent then used a sympathy appeal (*Stage 2*) to induce Tracy's care for him. After using a sympathy appeal, Vincent questioned Tracy about her plans for the day, and whom she was going to see. A common pattern in the relationship was for Vincent to instruct Tracy, often in a conciliatory tone, about what she should and should not be doing, thus attempting to control her whereabouts.

As heard in the following exchange between Vincent and Tracy focused on *Stages 2 and 3*, they were not arguing. Rather, their tone sounded conciliatory and soft, almost inaudibly soft.

Vincent: Good morning my love. (soft voice)
Tracy: Hi. How are you?
Vincent: Good. I just woke up.
Tracy: Well me too. Well. I showered but yeah.
Vincent: How are you?
Tracy: I miss you. [Connect over love/missing each other. Image of a solid connection.]
Vincent: What?
Tracy: I miss you.
Vincent: I love you too.
Tracy: I said I miss you.
Vincent: And I miss you too.
Tracy: (long pause) I'm okay. My throat is a little better today.
Vincent: Yeah.
(long pause)
Vincent: I'm really tired. I, I didn't get good sleep last night. [Sympathy appeal, intolerable jail conditions.]
Tracy: Why? Why?
Vincent: I, I, I don't know . . . um, just didn't get good sleep last night, you know, it's the stress Tuesday coming up—
Tracy: (interjects) What?
Vincent: I'm kind of stressed about Tuesday, you know? [Sympathy appeal. Tuesday was when Vincent was to appear in court for trial and sentencing.]
Tracy: Yah.
Vincent: I really want to be with you for your birthday. [Vincent presented love/care for Tracy and an image of a solid connection.]
Tracy: I hope you are. [Tracy responded with hope for a solid connection.]
(long pause)
Vincent: I love you.
Tracy: I love you, too.
(long pause)
Vincent: What are you doing today?

Vincent's jealousy about who Tracy was seeing while he was in jail was relentless. Vincent continued to ask Tracy to send cellphone photos to "prove" whom she was with. Only now, separated by the jail walls, Vincent asked in a conciliatory (i.e., rather than aggressive) tone.

While Tracy did not recant entirely about the abuse she suffered, she told the judge that Vincent's abuse was not as severe as the records indicated. Tracy reinforced to the court that she loved Vincent and wanted him to get professional help.

When Vincent got out of jail, he again accused Tracy of cheating on him and then physically assaulted her. Vincent said he would take his life by suicide if Tracy reported the abuse to the police.

When Vincent threatened suicide, Tracy communicated with a domestic violence advocate via text message. As illustrated in Figure 7.3, the professional advocate provided survivor-centered support; she validated Tracy's fears about Vincent attempting to kill himself and reinforced that Tracy was not at fault.

Vincent continued to try to reconcile with Tracy via text message, using apologies and promises of a better future. When Tracy would not reconcile, Vincent killed Tracy's cat. Vincent was then arrested and sentenced for further domestic violence crimes.

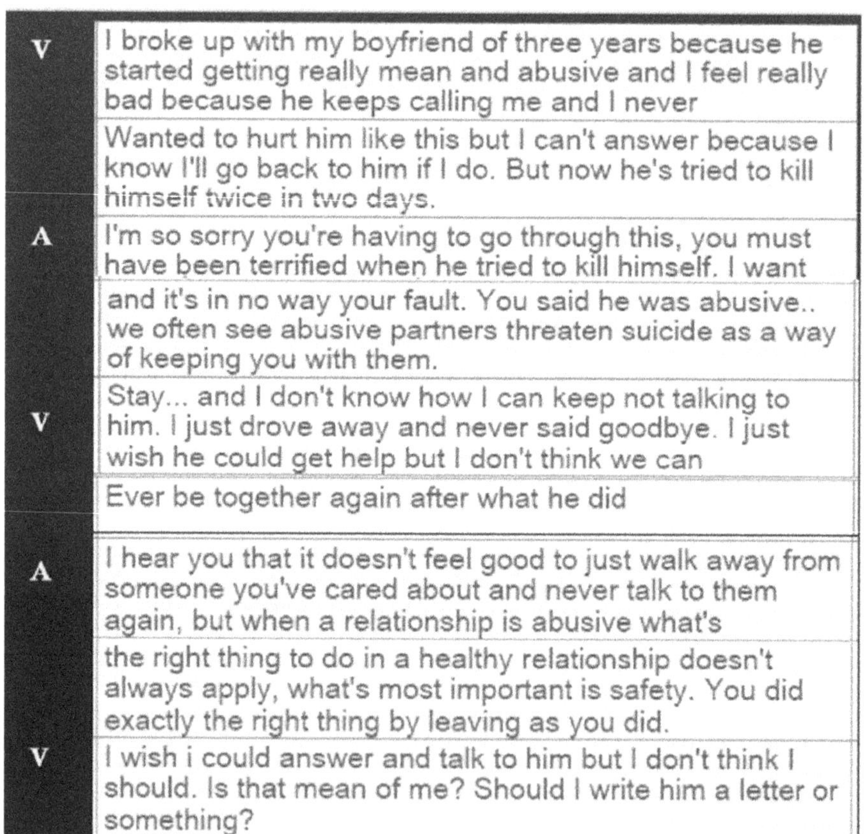

Figure 7.3 Tracy interacted with a domestic violence advocate via text message.

Summary

The case of Vincent and Tracy illustrates how Vincent supplemented jail calls (and moving through manipulations in the *five-stage model*) with text messages to tamper with Tracy after he was released from jail. While Tracy did not recant entirely about the abuse she suffered, she told the judge that Vincent's abuse was not as severe as the records indicated. Tracy reinforced to the court that she loved Vincent and wanted him to get professional help. When Vincent got out of jail, he accused Tracy of cheating on him, and he physically assaulted her. Vincent then said he would take his life by suicide if she reported the abuse to the police, threatened to harm her family members, and then killed Tracy's cat. Tracy electronically documented Vincent's abuse and used the support of professional advocates to move through prosecution efforts.

8 Your Mom Is Mean and Evil

Children growing up in homes where domestic violence occurs are witnesses to the abuse and are often used by abusers to further exploit their primary victim. Between 10 and 20 percent of children are exposed to domestic violence annually (Carlson, 2000) and are at increased risk of experiencing emotional, physical, and sexual abuse; of developing emotional and behavioral problems; and of having increased exposure to the presence of other adversities in their lives (Holt et al., 2008; Office of Juvenile Justice and Delinquency Prevention, 2021). When advising on an investigation or prosecution, or when providing expert testimony, we are routinely asked how abusers involve their children during jail calls to influence victim recantation (Bonomi and Martin, 2018). In this chapter, we use brief case examples to illustrate how abusers involve their children (directly and indirectly) during jail calls to further tamper with their primary victim. Because minors were involved in the conversations presented in the case examples, we did not include audio-recordings in this chapter. As the case examples in this chapter illustrate, abusers tend to use similar strategies with children during the jail calls as they do with their primary victim. These include minimizing the abuse and conjuring notions of a broken family and loss of emotional connection due to impending charges and sentencing (Bonomi et al., 2011). The use of children underscores an even more sophisticated level of abuse employed by the abuser by engaging the victim in weighing mutually exclusive and competing demands, i.e., preservation of the family versus holding a loved one accountable for ending their violence versus immediate and long-term safety and well-being.

Case 1: Bring "Our Son" to Court

Ron arrived home late one night and began harassing his wife Donna because he suspected she was cheating, though she said she wasn't.

When Donna attempted to breastfeed their infant son, Ron grabbed Donna and beat her until she lost consciousness. Ron had set a "rule" in the house that Donna could only feed their children when he said it was okay to do so.

Donna's teenage daughter from a prior relationship overheard the struggle and saw her mother being beaten while holding the baby. She called 911:

Operator: Nine-one-one, what are you reporting?
Teenage daughter: He's hitting her right now.
Operator: Okay . . . (unintelligible).
Teenage daughter: Like this is crazy.
Operator: Okay. And so caller can you—

DOI: 10.4324/9781003348696-9

Teenage daughter:	And her baby.
Operator:	Confirm the address?
Teenage daughter:	Her baby's in her hand and he keeps on hitting her.
Operator:	Okay. S-ma—

Police arrived shortly after the 911 call, and Ron was arrested at the scene. For context, Ron had at least a dozen prior domestic violence criminal convictions involving different victims and had more than 30 protection orders against him over his lifetime—in his relationship with Donna and with other women he had been intimately involved with.

In numerous calls that Ron made to Donna from jail, he ranted about the teenage daughter calling 911 and repeatedly demanded Donna say whatever would get him out of jail so he could return home and provide financially for the family (*Stages 3 and 4*) (Bonomi *et al.*, 2011).

Ron called his teenage (step-) daughter a "bitch" and a "snitch" for making the 911 call. "First of all, if—if your daughter wouldn't have a been a snitch, we wouldn't be in here." Donna said: "Okay. So she's—so basically my—so basically people are supposed ta just not care about what happens to me?"

Ron reminded Donna of her dependence on him and the role he played as caretaker of the family (*Stage 3*). Ron apologized but still resisted his role in the abuse (*Stage 1*).

Ron then reminded Donna of their infant son (whom he called "little man") and the implied loss of their "family" if he were to go to jail (*Stages 2 and 3*). Ron instructed Donna to appear in court with "little man" to effectively manipulate the judge to let Ron out of jail pending trial (*Stage 4*):

> You wanna sit there and think the baby is not a pawn. He's not a chess pawn. He's not a fuckin tool. I'm not gonna be pullin' [little man] back and forth in between us what we got goin' on. That's not right. . . . Me and you need to work on what we got goin' on because we're married, cause I got bills to pay. I gotta take care of my family. I'm not gonna sit there and watch my son [little man] not get what he wants or not get what we need. . . . We got a newborn kid and I gotta take care of my baby. These motherfuckers are gonna have to kill me cause they're not takin care of him. The only thing they want to do is tell you what to do with your family, but they don't want to give you any money to do it. . .. I love you and I'll see you (in court) tomorrow. You gotta be here with the baby.

Ron also made calls to his friends and family to help him manipulate Donna. In one call, he explained that he wanted to bring Donna money for milk for the baby. Ron said it is okay to bring Donna *some* money, around $100, but not to bring her "money-money." He did not want Donna to have a lot of money. He explained that he is the breadwinner in the family and that Donna cannot do anything without him.

In court, after being pressured repeatedly by Ron and reminded of what she stood to lose without Ron's financial support, Donna recanted. Donna stated that she lost her memory and did not remember what happened during the abuse event.

Case 2: Your Mom Is "Mean and Evil"

Michael severely beat his wife Kiara at a party because she was "ruining his chance to have fun." After a bystander called 911, the police arrived at the scene, chased after

Michael, and arrested him. Despite visible injuries, when questioned by the police, Kiara denied being beaten.

While awaiting trial, Michael called Kiara from jail and continued to abuse her, including attempting to use their seven-year-old daughter Brianna to manipulate Kiara.

During one of their jail calls, shortly after implicating Kiara in the abuse ("You sat there and wanted me to do that [break your nose]"—*Stage 1*), Michael asked to talk to their daughter Brianna. When Brianna got on the phone, Michael said the following:

> Your mom is mean and evil. Tell her I said that. Ask your mom why she hates me. Ask her why she don't love me, why she keep puttin' me in jail.

Brianna repeated the questions out loud. When Kiara returned from another room in the house, Kiara refused to give the phone back to Brianna. This prompted Michael to scream at Kiara repeatedly, "Can I talk to my [child]?!" [repeated multiple times]. Michael accused Kiara of being happy that he is in jail.

Shortly after Michael spoke with Brianna, he appealed to Kiara's sympathy by threatening suicide (*Stage 2*):

> Why you wanna kick a motherfucker while he's down, though? You're making me go crazy . . . you wanna seek a motherfucker suicidal?

Kiara exhibited strong agency during the calls (*Stage 1*), refusing to give in to Michael's pressure and manipulation. However, when Michael threatened suicide, Kiara became concerned and agreed to help him get out of jail (*Stage 2*). Kiara's susceptibility to Michael's sympathy appeal was reinforced by Michael's manipulation of their daughter.

Case 3: Dancing Naked Is Not Okay

In the third case, Trey arrived home intoxicated and attempted to suffocate Julie while she was asleep with their young child. Trey was arrested and made many calls to Julie from jail to influence her to recant her story.

During one of the jail calls, when Julie told Trey that his abuse is problematic, especially in front of their infant ("For you to treat me the way you do in front of [the infant], that's wrong"), Trey denied Julie's account. Trey conjured the idea that their infant, "come school age" would be ashamed of Julie's job as a dancer: "For you being a stripper is just wrong. If you're dancing naked in front of his [the baby's] schoolteacher, do you think that's going to be cool with him? Do you think it's going to be okay with him?"

Despite Julie's repeated attempts during the jail calls to make the case that she would not let their baby grow up in an abusive household, Trey blamed her for any "household dysfunction" and disparaged her role as a dancer: "Dancing naked in front of others . . . it does matter, it does matter."

Summary

As these three cases illustrate, the use of children directly or indirectly during jail calls is a technique domestic abusers use to tamper with and manipulate their victims. Abusers used similar strategies with children during jail calls as they did with their primary victims (e.g., minimizing the abuse, calling up images of a broken family due to impending charges and sentencing, engaging others to motivate recantation) (Bonomi *et al.*, 2011). The use of children in convincing a victim to recant her testimony underscores an even more callous type of abuse. The abuser engages the victim to consider competing scenarios. For example, the abuser might argue that the family should be kept together in the home to preserve the family as an alternative to having him removed.

References

Bonomi, A.E., R. Gangamma, C.R. Locke, H. Katafiasz, and D. Martin. 2011. "'Meet me at the hill where we used to park': Interpersonal processes associated with victim recantation." *Social Science and Medicine* 73: 1054–1061.

Bonomi, A.E., and D. Martin. 2018. "Jail calls: What do kids have to do with it." *Journal of Family Violence* 33 (2): 99–102.

Carlson, B.E. 2000. "Children exposed to intimate partner violence: Research findings and implications for intervention." *Trauma, Violence, & Abuse* 1 (4): 321–342.

Holt, S., H. Buckley, and S. Whelan. 2008. "The impact of exposure to domestic violence on children and young people: A review of the literature." *Child Abuse and Neglect* 32 (8): 797–810.

Office of Juvenile Justice and Delinquency Prevention. "Children exposed to violence. Literature review." *Model Programs Guide*. https://ojjdp.ojp.gov/model-programs-guide/literature-reviews/Children-Exposed-to-Violence.

Wyrick, P., and K. Atkinson. 2021. "Examining the relationship between childhood trauma and involvement in the justice system." *NIJ Journal* 283. https://nij.ojp.gov/topics/articles/examining-relationship-between-childhood-trauma-and-involvement-justice-system.

9 The *Five-Stage Model*, Jail Calls

Relationship to Coercive Control and Emotional Connection

Before jail recordings, practitioners relied on people's willingness to describe their experiences after domestic violence. Many victims were unable to share what happened after the abuse. Sharing was hard, unsafe, and often retraumatizing. Even when victims found the words, their recitation of abuse could be compromised by time and memory changes since the events, feelings of shame and worth associated with the abuse, and the editing and summarizing that happen with any retelling; no story is told exactly how it happened. Abusers rarely cooperated with requests to share their account of the situation, and when they did, they downplayed the abuse they inflicted and blamed the victims. Accounts can be further compromised by the skill, preconceptions, judgments, and biases of questioners. Attempts to create an objective and complete record of what occurred during and after abuse were almost impossible. Through an in-depth analysis of jail calls, our five-stage model illustrates a more nuanced understanding of domestic violence and coercive control—one that underscores a triumvirate of coercive control, sympathy appeals, and desire for the abuser and victim to emotionally reconnect, as evidenced in their jail-call conversations about everyday domestic situations.

Five-Stage Model: Extending an Understanding of Coercive Control

Coercive control is the process by which male partners employ gender-based (male) privilege to deprive women of their rights and liberties through domination (Stark, 2009). This includes the abuser limiting access to money and other resources. Women are especially vulnerable to coercive control because of their unequal political status in society, and because men can take advantage of their sexual inequalities (Anderson, 2009; Grace and Anderson, 2018).

Coercive control is understood as a key underlying dynamic of abusive relationships (Stark, 2009), cited globally throughout various courts. However, as currently conceptualized, coercive control has concentrated primarily on a one-way continuous coercive dynamic exerted by the abuser that disempowers victims. Coercive control could be further expanded to include some of the more nuanced second-by-second interpersonal dynamics we observed in the *five-stage model* through our study of the jail calls (Bonomi *et al.*, 2011). Some differences include how the couples' relationships are maintained through the abusers' sympathy appeals, their emotional connection, and the couples' united positioning against others who they believed could not understand their relationship (Bonomi *et al.*, 2011).

In the case examples in this book, abusers (all of whom had an immediate motive to get released from jail) spoke at length with victims using mixed strategies. Not only did abusers employ sophisticated techniques (within the framework of coercive control) to manipulate, for power and control, or get out from under the threat of prosecution, they pressured

DOI: 10.4324/9781003348696-10

their victims to preserve and maintain the relationships through many hours of conversation about ordinary matters, thereby coercing the victims to feel dependent. As we noted in Chapter 3, an abuser's manipulation of the victim is so successful in part because they are pressuring the victim to engage in normative behavior (to remain in and maintain the relationship), even though the relationship is characterized by significant harm. This aligns with a family systems orientation (Bowen, 1985) and with human attachment (to be loved) theory (Bowlby, 1973), which helps to explain couples remaining emotionally connected.

The jail calls revealed many discussions between the abuser and victim about everyday issues, such as how their day went. Conversations between a victim and abuser resemble that of any other couple. Recall the couple in Chapter 7 whose soft-spoken exchange (barely above a whisper) focused on how restful their night's sleep was and how they missed each other. Or the couple in Chapter 2 who discussed getting tattoos of each other's names. Or the couple in Chapter 5 who listened to a song—which conjured memories of their earlier times together and reinforced the tenuousness of their relationship while the abuser was in jail. In Chapter 3, which summarized the strengths and limitations of the *five-stage model*, we referred to these strategies as the abuser attempting to normalize the relationship and their interactions—despite the severe violence abusers had inflicted.

Abusers' manipulation was not a part of every conversation. Sometimes we were surprised by how infrequently the criminal case was discussed between the abuser and victim; couples went on living the normal parts of their lives despite the legal case. The relationship between victim and abuser included abuse, but also togetherness, familiarity, and connection.

Our analyses and case examples using jail calls demonstrate that current understandings of domestic violence and coercive control are incomplete—not just about how and why victims recant or disengage from prosecution of their abuser but about the entirety of how abusive relationships function. Abusers use highly sophisticated techniques to minimize the abuse they inflict and to manipulate the victim. Our research corroborates and builds upon the understanding that victims are both agentic and susceptible to abuser manipulation.

Couples' Bonding Over Emotional Connection: Controversial in the Field

Our discovery that victim recantation was related to the couples' emotional connection or continued attachment was initially controversial. When we presented to audiences globally, there were always a handful of people who questioned that victims would want to remain emotionally connected to their abuser and that abusers shared a similar desire. However, the conclusion that emotional connection is a core of abusive relationships and linked to recantation was validated in Kernic *et al.*'s (2023) epidemiological study of case files involving couples with a criminally involved domestic abuser. In Kernic *et al.*'s study, emotional connection was a strong driver of recantation. Specifically, victims engaged in complex and intense emotional attachment or caretaking were more likely than other victims to recant or disengage from prosecution. Kernic *et al.*'s findings are consistent with Cala *et al.*'s (2015) findings that victims who remained in contact with their abuser or who had thoughts of reconciliation were more likely than other victims to disengage from prosecution efforts.

Our concept that couples remained bonded emotionally was not the only controversy. Some experts dismissed our *five-stage model* and the jail calls believing there was nothing new about the discovery. Some experts questioned the reality and legitimacy of the jail calls, believing the calls hid the threats and coercion that are constant in violent relationships. The absence of direct threats during the jail calls did not mean threats were nonexistent; clearly, the threat of future violence posed a constant underlying stressor. And, while each victim clearly faced the risk of future abuse, our research showed that more than any other tactic, abusers used subtle strategies during jail calls, such as sympathy appeals, to influence victims to recant.

Experts were not wrong to question the *five-stage model* and our analysis of jail calls, especially with the new discoveries that changed what is known about domestic violence and coercive control. However, as is human nature, experts might have allowed prior biases to drive their interpretations of what they considered valid and invalid about relationship dynamics. Our original study used constructivist grounded theory (Charmaz, 2006) as a qualitative theoretical lens, which allowed us to honor existing theories of domestic violence as a dynamic of patriarchal and coercive control (Pence and Paymar, 1993; Stark, 2009) while allowing for novel discoveries about the couples' interpersonal relationship dynamic, including the role that emotional connection played (Bonomi *et al.*, 2011). This allowed our team to bridge an understanding of how patriarchal and coercive control (Pence and Paymar, 1993; Stark, 2009) and emotional connectivity (Bowen, 1985; Bowlby, 1973; Gangamma and Bonomi, 2010) operate in violent relationships.

Sympathy Appeals: Shifting the Abuser Into the Role of "Victim"

Our discovery that abusers used sympathy appeals to manipulate care and concern from the victim was not new. However, our illustration of how abusers enacted sympathy appeals during jail conversations with victims had not been shown before in the field. We were able to hear exactly what abusers said, how they said it, and how victims responded. Perhaps the reason sympathy appeals worked so well in shifting a victim's emotions is that they prey on the victim's empathy and also their desire to be cared for. To desire these qualities is a natural part of being human. At the core of Bowlby's foundational work on human attachment is the longing to belong and to be connected in relationships. Taken together, our results show a more nuanced picture of abusive relationships: a triumvirate of coercive control, sympathy appeals, and desire for connection in relationships grounded in everyday conversations.

Listening to Jail Calls: "Shocking"

When presenting our findings to professional audiences, we routinely hear that they are "shocked" to hear what the jail calls sound like—what abusers say, how they say it, and how victims respond. For years, professionals heard from victims what abusers said; but for the first time during jail calls, they heard the actual dialogue.

Unlike conducting interviews or reading victim impact statements, jail calls put the listener inside the story of abuse—hearing the tone, context, and expressions used in a call between two people in an abusive relationship. Jail calls capture the feelings of abusers and victims that are frequently lost in retellings: fear, anger, grief, and heartbreak. Recordings provide a much deeper understanding of the exchange, as even the best storyteller leaves out details.

Listening to Jail Calls: "Facing Ourselves, Our Own Relationships"

When listening to jail calls, we are frequently faced with reexamining our own relationships. When teaching the *five-stage model* with audio-recorded jail calls at the Ohio State

University, one student came after class to say she decided to leave her boyfriend after hearing the calls and seeing that her relationship was unhealthy. In another teaching venue using the jail recordings, some students recognized a few unhealthy tendencies in their own relationships. They requested we start a clinically supervised peer support group to talk through what constitutes healthy and unhealthy relationships. It is possible that the "shock" professional audiences shared with us when listening to the audiotapes stemmed from recognizing the realities of relationship patterns in the lives of those they care about. However, interviews with those professional audiences would be needed to explore that idea.

Conclusions

Before jail recordings, practitioners relied on people's willingness to describe their experiences of domestic violence. After being abused, many victims were unwilling or unable to share what had happened. Sharing could be difficult, feel unsafe, and often retraumatize the victim. Abusers rarely responded to requests to share their accounts of the situations. Accounts can be further compromised by the skill, preconceptions, judgments, and biases of questioners. Attempts to create an objective and complete written record of what occurred during and after abuse were almost impossible. Through an in-depth analysis of jail calls, we developed a *five-stage model* to illustrate a more nuanced understanding of domestic violence and coercive control—one that underscores a triumvirate of coercive control, sympathy appeals, and desire for emotional connection through relationships grounded in everyday conversations between abusers and victims.

Our book comes approximately a decade after our first jail-call study (Bonomi *et al.*, 2011) and more than 15 years since jail recordings became available. There has been no other published research using jail conversations apart from our follow-up publications. Many hours of recorded jail-call conversations between abusers and victims are available to examine, along with other media formats such as video calls between abusers and victims. We hope that the work in this book will not only expand an understanding of domestic violence and recantation but also inspire further inquiry into the *five-stage model*, jail calls, and new media formats (e.g., video calls).

In Chapter 10, we offer recommendations for how our work could be used to improve community response to domestic violence. For example, for educators and students, there may be no better instructional tool to teach about the dynamics of domestic violence and coercive control than supervised listening to jail calls. In classes at the Ohio State University, graduate students (after obtaining approval from the human subjects' ethics committee) selected one couple from our jail-call study (Bonomi *et al.*, 2011) to study throughout the semester. They used the *five-stage model* to compare what they heard in the recordings using existing domestic violence theories ranging from patriarchal and coercive control (Pence and Paymar, 1993; Stark, 2009) to family systems (Bowen, 1985) to attachment (Bowlby, 1973).

References

Anderson, K.L. 2009. "Gendering coercive control." *Violence Against Women* 15 (12): 1444–1457.

Bonomi, A.E., R. Gangamma, C.R. Locke, H. Katafiasz, and D. Martin. 2011. "'Meet me at the hill where we used to park': Interpersonal processes associated with victim recantation." *Social Science and Medicine* 73: 1054–1061.

Bonomi, A.E., and D. Martin. 2018. "Jail calls: What do kids have to do with it." *Journal of Family Violence* 33 (2): 99–102.

Bowen, M. 1985. "On the differentiation of self (1972)." In *Family Therapy in Clinical Practice*, 478. Lanham, MD: Rowman & Littlefield Publishers.

Bowlby, J. 1973. *Separation: Anxiety & Anger. Attachment and Loss* (vol. 2, International psycho-analytical library no. 95). London: Hogarth Press.

Cala, M., M.E. Trigo, and F.J. Saavedra. 2016. "Women's disengagement from legal proceedings for intimate partner violence: Sociodemographic and psychological variables." *European Journal of Psychology Applied to Legal Context* 8: 35–42.

Charmaz, K. 2006. *Constructing Grounded Theory: A Practical Guide Through Qualitative Analysis*. London: Sage Publications.

Gangamma, R., and A.E. Bonomi. 2010. "Developing a systemic interpretation of couple-level data." Paper presented at the Advances in Qualitative Methods Conference, Vancouver, BC.

Grace, K.T., and J.C. Anderson. 2018. "Reproductive coercion: A systematic review." *Trauma, Violence & Abuse* 19 (4): 371–390.

Kernic, M., L. Drolette, S. Shanahan, and D. Martin. 2023. *Victim Recantation and Disengagement from Prosecution in Intimate Partner Violence Criminally Prosecuted Crimes in King County*. Washington, DC: Predictors of Victim Recantation and Disengagement and Prosecutorial Outcomes. U.S. Department of Justice, National Institute of Justice (Grant #: 2017-VA-CX-0034).

Pence, E., and M. Paymar. 1993. *Education Groups for Men Who Batter: The Duluth Model*. New York: Springer Publishing Company.

Stark, E. 2009. *Coercive Control: The Entrapment of Women in Personal Life*. Oxford: Oxford University Press.

10 Using the *Five-Stage Model* and Jail Calls to Advance Community Response to Domestic Violence

Expert Testimony

The *five-stage model* and jail calls have been used globally to educate courts and juries about the dynamics of domestic violence and recantation. The *five-stage model* supports well-established tools such as the Power and Control Wheel (Figure 10.1) to show how victims are tampered with and manipulated. Expert witnesses often include victim advocates, clinicians, and researchers with knowledge and understanding of domestic violence dynamics and impacts.

When expert witnesses use the *five-stage model* and jail calls when providing their testimony, the process typically involves the following steps. The prosecutor directs the expert witness to describe the dynamics of domestic violence and how abuse impacts the health and well-being of victims. The prosecutor displays the Power and Control Wheel as an "exhibit"—that is, evidence to be considered by the jury (Figure 10.1). Expert witnesses walk the jury through each segment of the Power and Control Wheel, providing abuse examples in each segment. If the victim in the case identifies as a member of a minoritized group, the expert witness provides evidence-based information about how impacts and structural barriers are often amplified for such victims. For example, when providing expert testimony to support victims who identify as Indigenous, the expert witness discusses how abuse in Indigenous communities is elevated as compared to non-Indigenous communities and how geographic barriers often hamper the ability of Indigenous victims to access services they need.

After reviewing the Power and Control Wheel, expert testimony then transitions to describe the dynamics of victim recantation. The expert witness walks the jury through the *five-stage model*, emphasizing the following as key features in each stage:

Stage 1: Arguing and resistance of each other's accounts
Stage 2: Sympathy appeals
Stage 3: Bonding
Stage 4: Abuser asks victim to recant, reinforced with sympathy appeals
Stage 5: Couple works together on the recantation plan

After the expert witness testifies, the prosecution team plays jail calls (if jail calls are available) from the case for the jury. The jail calls illustrate how the abuser tampered with and manipulated the victim and how the couple moved through the five stages.

On occasion, defense attorneys may ask the expert witness whether all "spokes" (i.e., stages) of the *five-stage model* need to be in place for recantation to occur. It is an important and relevant question. Just as not every abuse element needs to be present in the

DOI: 10.4324/9781003348696-11

Figure 10.1 Duluth Power and Control Wheel.

Source: Reprinted from PowerandControl.pdf (https://www.theduluthmodel.org/wp-content/uploads/2017/03/PowerandControl.pdf).

Power and Control Wheel for abuse to be occurring, not every stage of the *five-stage model* needs to be present for an abuser's tampering to influence a victim's recantation. For example, sometimes within the *five-stage model* (and as illustrated in the cases presented in our book), couples will spend more time in *Stage 3* (bonding over earlier, happier times), whereas other couples may spend less time on these topics.

Education and Training in Universities

The *five-stage model* and jail calls have been used to advance understanding of the dynamics of domestic violence with university students training to be clinicians. In classes at the Ohio State University, graduate students enrolled in Amy's class *Violent Family Systems* selected the jail calls of one couple in the original jail-call study (Bonomi *et al.*, 2011) to interact with throughout the semester. Graduate students compared what they heard in the jail calls to domestic violence theories (of their choice), such as patriarchal control (Pence and Paymar, 1993), family systems (Bowen, 1985; Gangamma and Bonomi, 2010), and attachment (Allison *et al.*, 2008; Bartholomew and Allison, 2006; Bowlby, 1973). The jail calls helped students understand the tone, context, and emotions—in ways that clinical interactions in therapeutic settings cannot often reveal due to the clinician's presence.

victims have shared with us, they are being so heavily manipulated by their abusers that it often takes years for victims to see and understand what is happening.

Prosecution

Use of the *five-stage model* and jail calls could lead to more informed prosecution, case disposition, and trials. For prosecutors, jail calls represent compelling evidence of witness tampering and manipulation. Case law now regularly details the use of recorded jail calls by prosecutors to expose abuser manipulation. Jail calls are relevant evidence of consciousness of guilt where abusers often freely acknowledge the abuse. Jail calls also allow prosecutors to demonstrate "forfeiture by wrongdoing," which is when an abuser engages in wrongdoing to prevent witnesses against them from testifying; the law permits the admission of evidence over the abuser's right to confrontation. Jail calls also defeat attempts to excuse abuse because they belie abusers' fabricated claims of mental illness, self-defense, or false alibi (Wilkinson *et al.*, 2016).

In court, jail calls are persuasive evidence of not just what the abuser says but how they say it. Abusers aim to project a carefully constructed image of themselves as peaceful, responsible, and wrongfully accused, while suggesting the victim is to blame. When prosecutors play recorded jail calls in court, the abuser's "peaceful" image is shattered; abusers' relentless tone and tenor of manipulation are heard, as are victims' agency and empathy. The jail calls demonstrate how victims are drawn into the *five-stage model.*

Knowing that abusers' manipulation is frequently associated with victim recantation and disengagement, even in cases where there are no jail-call recordings (e.g., the many instances where abusers are not in custody), prosecutors should redouble their efforts to analyze how to proceed. Abusers are distinguished by their willingness to subvert the legal system, conduct a campaign of sophisticated tampering, and disobey court orders.

Jail calls, thoroughly researched using the *five-stage model*, also provide a framework for prosecutors to strengthen their approach outside the courtroom. Traditionally, victims who recant are seen as disinterested, and their services are then deprioritized. Jail calls act as a catalyst for how to think about victims who recant and abusers who manipulate. When professionals understand the dynamics of recantation, they can assure that comprehensive victim services are provided (Association of Prosecuting Attorneys Position Statement), including utilizing highly effective comprehensive service Family Justice Centers (Hellman *et al.*, 2007; Murray *et al.*, 2020a).

For prosecutors, recorded jail calls and the *five-stage model* also provide additional means to uncover and respond to "victim-defendants." There is a long-standing problem with victims being improperly arrested by police during domestic violence investigations. This happens when abusers claim to be the victim. As this book details, many abusers are expert manipulators, so it is no surprise they can mislead police as to what occurred. Recorded jail conversations reveal how abusers manipulate police to frame victims. The abuser himself provides evidence of his manipulation when he talks to his victim from jail; we hear this on jail-call recordings and analyze them using our *five-stage model.*

References

Allison, C.J., K. Bartholomew, O. Mayseless, and D.G. Dutton. 2008. "Love as a battlefield: Dynamics in couples identified for male partner violence." *Journal of Family Issues* 20 (1): 125–150.

Association of Prosecuting Attorneys Domestic Violence Committee Position Statement. www.apainc.org/wp-content/uploads/2020/11/APA-Policy-Statement-DV-Committee-Position.pdf.

Bartholomew, K., and C.J. Allison. 2006. "An attachment perspective on abusive dynamics in intimate relationships." In *Dynamics of Romantic Love: Attachment, Caregiving, and Sex*, edited by M. Mikulincer and G.S. Goodman, 102–127. New York: Guilford.

Berliner, L., L. Merchant, A. Roberts, and D. Martin. 2020. "Cognitive behavioral therapy for intimate partner violence." www.dshs.wa.gov/sites/default/files/ESA/csd/documents/dv/CBT%20for%20IPV%20Guide%20with%20Handouts%20UW%20Harborview%20Curriculum.pdf.

Bonomi, A.E., R. Gangamma, C.R. Locke, H. Katafiasz, and D. Martin. 2011. "'Meet me at the hill where we used to park': Interpersonal processes associated with victim recantation." *Social Science and Medicine* 73: 1054–1061.

Bonomi, A.E., and D. Martin. 2018. "Jail calls: What do kids have to do with it." *Journal of Family Violence* 33 (2): 99–102.

Bowen, M. 1985. "On the differentiation of self (1972)." In *Family Therapy in Clinical Practice*, 478. Lanham, MD: Rowman & Littlefield Publishers.

Bowlby, J. 1973. *Separation: Anxiety & Anger. Attachment and Loss* (vol. 2, International psychoanalytical library no. 95). London: Hogarth Press.

Effiong, J.E., P.N. Ibeagha, and S.K. Iorfa. 2022. "Traumatic bonding in victims of intimate partner violence is intensified via empathy." *Journal of Social Personal Relationships* 39 (12): 3619–3637.

Ferrari, G., G. Feder, R. Agnew-Davies, J.E. Bailey, S. Hollinghurst, L. Howard, E. Howarth, L. Sardinha, D. Sharp, and T.J. Peters. 2018. "Psychological advocacy towards healing (PATH): A randomized controlled trial of a psychological intervention in a domestic violence service setting." *PLoS One* 13 (11): e0205485.

Gangamma, R., and A.E. Bonomi. 2010. "Developing a systemic interpretation of couple-level data." Paper presented at the Advances in Qualitative Methods Conference, Vancouver, BC.

Hellman, C.M., G. Casey, G. Gwinn. Strack, M.B, Muñoz, R.T., Brady, S.R. Aguirre, N. Aceves, Y. 2007. *Nurturing Hope and Well-Being among Survivors of Domestic Violence within the Family Justice Center Model.* The President's Family Justice Center Initiative, Department of Justice.

Kuskoff, E., C. Parsell, S. Plage, F. Perales, and C. Ablaza. 2023. "Of good mothers and violent fathers: Negotiating child protection interventions in abusive relationships." *Violence Against Women.* February 22, online ahead of print.

Murray, C., A. Lay, B. Wyche, and C. Johnson. 2020a. "Professionals' perceptions of the impact of a family justice center: A four-year, cross-sectional study." *Journal of Aggression, Conflict and Peace Research* 12 (4): 223–238.

Murray, L.K., J.C. Kane, N. Glass, S.S. van Wyk, F. Melendez, R. Paul, C.K. Danielson, S.M. Murray, J. Mayeya, F. Simenda, and P. Bolton. 2020b. "Effectiveness of the common elements treatment approach (CETA) in reducing intimate partner violence and hazardous alcohol use in Zambia (VATU): A randomized controlled trial." *PLoS Medicine* 17 (4): e1003056.

Office of Justice Programs. "New approaches to policing high-risk intimate partner victims and those committing the crimes." *National Institute of Justice.* https://ojp.gov.

Pence, E., and M. Paymar. 1993. *Education Groups for Men Who Batter: The Duluth Model.* New York: Springer Publishing Company.

Petersen, K., R.C. Davis, and B.G. Taylor. 2022. "Effects of second responder programs on repeat incidents of family abuse: An updated systematic review and meta-analysis." *Campbell System Review* 18 (1): 1–37.

Rubenstein, B.Y., M.L.T. Wojcik, V.R. Anderson, and B.S. Fisher. 2021. "Shifting the service referral paradigm using community-based second responders: Examining weapon use in intimate partner violence." *Journal of Family Violence* 36: 527–535.

U.S. Department of Justice. 2013. *Evaluation of the Abuser Focused Domestic Violence Initiative (OFDVI) in High Point, NC, and Replication in Lexington, NC* (Final report for Community

Oriented Policing Services, Cooperative Agreement Number 2013-CK-WX-K028). Washington, DC: U.S. Department of Justice.

Wilkinson, J., F. Cruz, H. Furman, and S. Kennedy. 2016. "Combatting witness intimidation: Experiences in creating systems-based change (Aequitas, Microsoft Word—CWI Final Report 9.26.19.docx)." aequitasresource.org.

Epilogue

Amy Bonomi

Each couple we have interacted with over the years has a profoundly unique and impactful story—a story containing hope, heartache, loss, despair, trauma, resilience, strength, and recovery. Through the jail calls, we witnessed the second-by-second ebb and flow of emotions and behaviors within those stories. We hope that our book has facilitated readers and listeners to connect to those profound and impactful stories in ways that expand understanding.

In writing our book, and in our original jail-call study, we faced many difficult choices. Whose stories would we write about? How would we come to a consensus on which jail calls would be both most illustrative of the *five-stage model* and impactful for listeners?

Our choices were especially difficult because we felt every second of conversation warranted a page in the book and in our jail-call publication. Every jail-call conversation bore significant meaning. Every exchange helped to illustrate the *five-stage model*.

We ultimately decided to reflect a blend of information from and across couples (with altered details)—an approach commonly used in therapeutic training settings to protect confidentiality and safety.

We considered including a few long-form jail calls in the book—that is, longer audiotaped jail calls that formed the basis of our original 2011 publication. However, we worried that including the long-form calls without a supportive context for debriefing could be emotionally jarring for listeners. Our work has shown that navigating the long-form jail calls requires a supportive context for the listener. Recall the graduate students (training to be clinicians) who described feeling a "tower of anxiety" when interacting with the jail calls and their need for a clinical community (our class) to process. In one class activity, students depicted the "tower of anxiety" by stacking balls of clay (Figure E.1). Throughout our class activities, we processed students' feelings and reactions together in a supportive class community.

In addition, when working on our original 2011 study (which culminated in the *five-stage model* of recantation), weekly team meetings were paramount to help team members process secondary trauma that resulted from listening to the long-form jail calls.

In our case examples (Chapters 4 through 8), we considered including more details about the abuse scene. For example, we pondered including the public-record 911 call that Amanda made to police while John was abusing her (Chapter 4). On the one hand, Amanda's 911 call would put the listener in touch with some of the terror that Amanda and her young child faced. On the other hand, the 911 call could be too jarring for

DOI: 10.4324/9781003348696-12

Figure E.1 Students depicted a "tower of anxiety" from interacting with the jail calls.

listeners. It took several days for our team to process the impact of hearing Amanda's 911 call for the first time.

We could have included more details about abusers in the book. One abuser rendered many nuanced paintings reflecting his emotional state and stance toward women, including his feelings about the victim he abused. Dr Rashmi Gangamma and I included some of these additional contextual details when writing our narrative summaries in our 2011 jail-call study (described in Chapter 2).

Each of these details are important. Each detail helps us understand the stories and processes of domestic violence better. The details help us understand victims better. Understand abusers better. Understand humanity better.

As John and Amanda's jail call illustrates (Audio E.1), there are many more details and many more stories to listen to, to hear, to understand. There is much more to be analyzed to advance an understanding of prevention and response to domestic violence. We encourage listeners who are interested in interacting with more jail calls to seek research-practitioner partnerships on these data. There is a mountain of research to be undertaken using the jail-call data (along with cellular phone extractions, social media, and body-worn camera footage).

Further analysis of jail calls could reveal important details about how couples feel about treatment. How and where could domestic violence advocates best intervene to interrupt abuser tampering and manipulation? We observed an effective text message exchange between a domestic violence advocate and victim in Chapter 6. How and where else could those helpful interactions occur?

Jail calls could also be analyzed through any number of theoretical and interpretive lenses. Intersectionality, for example: how do abusers exploit victims' minoritized identities during jail calls (if at all) to influence their recantation (Crenshaw, 1989)? Traumatic bonding, as another example: could jail calls help explicate the role that traumatic bonding has in influencing recantation (Effiong *et al.*, 2022)? Comparing and contrasting interpretive (qualitative) analysis lenses, as another example (Starks and Trinidad, 2007).

There are endless analysis possibilities. There are endless stories to be listened to, heard, and responded to. We hope others join us on these pathways.

David Martin

Every day I walk into the King County Courthouse, I pass through metal detectors. The metal detectors were installed in 1995 after the most public domestic violence homicide in the history of my community: an abuser murdered his wife (who was pregnant) and her two friends outside a courtroom. Now, a plaque sits next to the metal detectors in memory of the victims (Figure E.2). It reads, "There is no excuse for domestic violence." People still lay flowers on it to this day.

Figure E.2 Plaque in memory of victims

I started working as a prosecutor in 1996, a year after the metal detectors and the plaque were installed. The courthouse is much the same.

While the courthouse itself is much the same, the landscape of domestic violence has changed. In 1996, domestic violence prosecution was not a popular or prioritized area. As a new prosecutor, when I asked to only work on domestic violence cases, my request was met with surprise. Domestic violence was thought of as a pain, the type of case to avoid. Now years later, perceptions have changed: domestic violence is seen and addressed as a critically important matter of community public health and safety.

The passage of strong laws made a difference. The Violence Against Women Act provided national laws and funding. Multinational treaties were signed on violence against women abroad. Strangulation became a serious offense. Juries were permitted to hear about prior acts of domestic violence to help explain why victims recanted (e.g., *State v. Grant*, 83 Wn. App. 98, 1996).

Family Justice Centers formed. Funding grew for community-based domestic violence organizations. In King County, where I do most of my work, the domestic violence homicide rate dropped from 29 deaths a year in 1980 to 14 deaths in 2022, all while the population doubled in size.

Many organizations and individuals raised awareness and resources to address domestic violence. Organizations like New Beginnings in Washington State were places of inspiration in combatting domestic violence. Their work inspired shifts in culture. They showed the critical importance of community involvement in addressing domestic violence and how individuals can make a difference by supporting local organizations and advocating for change.

There was growth in public health research to understand domestic violence as an indicator driving violent crime and death. The public health approach integrated parallel strategies of data-informed policies and community health practices to examine the cultural and structural barriers that reinforced the cycle of abuse.

The domestic violence continuum of approaches also expanded to include school-based partnerships as examples of prevention methods to raise awareness of the types of manipulation that occur in abusive relationships.

My office joined others in creating a specialized court and domestic violence unit to focus only on domestic violence cases.

Having trained professional audiences internationally, as a part of the U.S. Fulbright program, I see the cultural and structural changes in domestic violence from local to global efforts aimed at building a continuum of prevention and intervention strategies. Cross-cultural education, international convenings, and collaborative and multidisciplinary practitioner exchange programs have allowed for sharing important policy and program models, leading to adaptations and new solutions to end domestic violence.

Yet, despite all the positive developments, domestic violence persists. The flow of egregious abuse cases has no end. While aspects of professional culture around domestic violence have moved forward, there remains a paucity of resources and support for victims. In court, victims are frequently alone, accompanied only by advocates. Abusers are often surrounded by friends, family, and community. In one case my unit worked on, dozens of people from a church community came to support an abuser, while the victim was accompanied only by the domestic violence advocate on the other side of the courtroom. Jury trials subject victims to bias and unfair scrutiny. The cycle of intimidation exists systemically for victims.

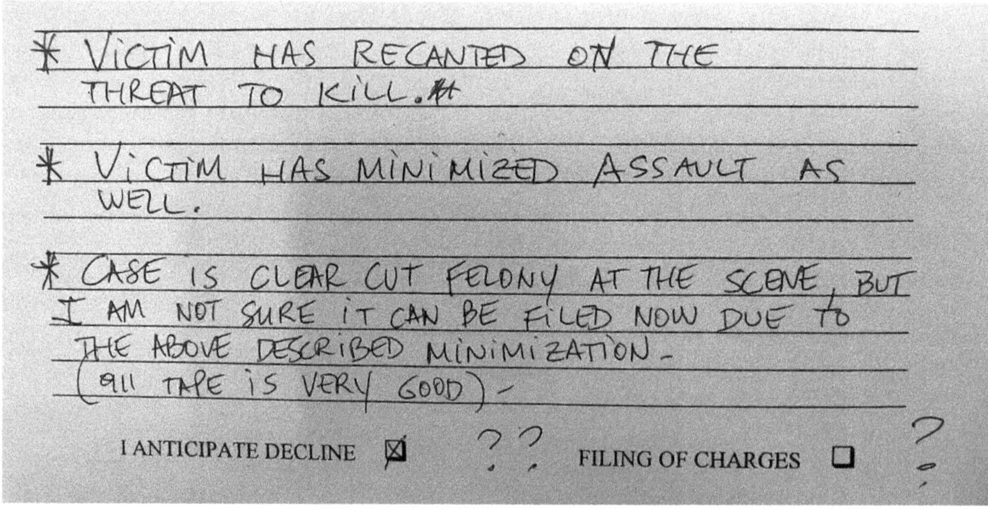

* VICTIM HAS RECANTED ON THE THREAT TO KILL. *

* VICTIM HAS MINIMIZED ASSAULT AS WELL.

* CASE IS CLEAR CUT FELONY AT THE SCENE, BUT I AM NOT SURE IT CAN BE FILED NOW DUE TO THE ABOVE DESCRIBED MINIMIZATION. (911 TAPE IS VERY GOOD) -

I ANTICIPATE DECLINE ☒ ?? FILING OF CHARGES ☐ ?

Figure E.3 Handwritten notes of case involving John and Amanda.

Children are ever present in domestic violence and have few resources available to them. My office has observed that those same children grow up and become abusers and victims themselves. I have done this work long enough that I have seen a generational pattern: I have prosecuted the sons of abusers whom I prosecuted years ago.

Domestic violence work takes a toll. Every case is heartbreaking. There are long hours, high caseloads, unending stress, and secondary trauma.

What helps in navigating the heavy toll of domestic violence is readily available information to help us prosecute cases. When I first started as a prosecutor, police reports, cassette tapes of 911 calls, and maybe some photographs were all kept in paper files. Today, electronic records management systems detail abusive relationships through recorded jail conversations, cellular phone extractions, social media, and body-worn camera footage.

Jail calls signaled evidence of witness tampering and manipulation and increased legal accountability for abusers. I remember the first time I listened to jail calls in Amanda and John's case, discussed in the Preface and Chapter 4. Hearing John's voice at the beginning of his call to Amanda, saying, "[t]his is where you think I need to be," felt like battering distilled. John's words filled with coercive, controlling, defiant anger and blame shifting. I will never forget what I felt. I understood John in a way no police report, victim statement, court testimony, or classroom could ever do. I had the same feeling many have hearing jail calls for the first time—the instant recognition of tampering and manipulation.

While going through John's old paper case file while writing our book, I was reminded that John's case was almost not charged. The investigating detective had questioned whether it was viable (Figure E.3). My file note debated the case with a colleague, which read: "He threatens to kill V and bites her face, D wakes V up by assaulting her, strikes and bites her, strangles her. Interferences with reporting. 911 tape is raw emotion, D has likely prior in a different court, apparently with V. There was a child present for incident, can aggravate. Need to have a felony here."

My note made me think about how many other domestic violence cases were not pursued, how manipulation is deeply ingrained in cases, and how many victims do not receive the justice they deserve.

John and Amanda's case also reminds me of how it ended. Despite pleading to more charges, spending a longer time in custody, and going to treatment, John abused Amanda. He intimidated her for years. John was in and out of domestic violence and substance abuse treatment. One recorded jail call involved John and Amanda discussing treatment and relationship counseling. Amanda believed John would never stop abusing her, and John claimed that she was abusive with her words (see also Chapter 4). Amanda and John did not believe in treatment but believed it was their last shot, a reminder of the heartbreaking complexity of domestic violence cases.

John: Hey, what are you doing?
Amanda: Just cleaning up a little bit.
John: What's wrong? You said, why, baby? I'm sorry. What's, what are you thinking about?
Amanda: I just want to have normal days to get along and be happy, you know, and it's never gonna happen ever. It's sad.
John: Why isn't it gonna happen?
Amanda: Because . . . You won't stop now. You'll never stop. And that's why makes me so depressed that I feel like you'll never stop no matter what. You'll go to these bullshit classes. They're gonna order you to go to and you're not even gonna fucking pay attention. You know?
John: Pretty much.
Amanda: Yeah. Well I don't have anything to say to you.
John: Why are you fucking funny now? We just got through talking.
Amanda: Yeah, well, you recognize it. You do have a domestic problem.
John: I know, but you got a verbal abuse problem that leads me to lose my temper. You gotta understand that you know, your, your words, the things that you say upset me a lot. Things that you say to me and you know, I, I understand I do the same thing to you, but you know, that's—
Amanda: It's like ten times worse though. I mean, I just defend myself.
John: No, a lot of the times. Your words just, you know, you say stuff that you shouldn't be saying? You know, just stuff out of the blue that you'll say that'll make me mad and upset. Not to say that I do anything that, you know, like I'm an angel. I'm not. I'm just saying we need to go to counseling together. Relationship counseling is what we need.
Amanda: I agree. But is it even worth going? You're gonna intimidate me to hurt me all the time. Will it work you think?
John: It doesn't hurt to try it. It'll most likely be our last shot. Uh, trying to salvage our, what we have. You know what I'm saying? It's always worth the try, I guess. I mean, it doesn't hurt to go there and hear somebody else's opinion who went to school and specialized in, you know, relationships. You know, it, it, it doesn't hurt to talk to him. I mean, regardless if we learn anything or not, it doesn't have to try to save what we have and continue our future with baby.

Years after John continued to abuse Amanda, and after they had more children together, I wondered if I could have done anything different. I realize that every decision and option in John and Amanda's relationship was clouded by John's manipulation. Was treatment for someone like John too difficult? Did he truly have the capacity to change? Would knowledge of the *five-stage model* have made a difference? If Amanda had worked with a victim advocate who exposed her to the *five-stage model*, would Amanda have recanted? If John's treatment for his abuse exposed him to the *five-stage model*, would John and Amanda's story have had a different ending?

There are no easy choices and no easy answers in Amanda and John's case. The reality is that we still do not understand completely enough the choices that victims and abusers make. That is why I felt compelled to share the recorded calls with Amy years ago, and why Amy and I wrote this book.

Amy's formative work on the jail calls and our subsequent work together push us toward deeper engagement with domestic violence as a community public health and safety issue. Our work has revealed new additional insights and understanding of why domestic violence must be approached comprehensively. Recorded jail calls are a microcosm of the macro problems of gender-based violence and help to demonstrate common patterns in abuse worldwide. The consistent patterns of recantation identified in Amy's research and our continued work together are shared across communities to raise awareness. We heard from professional audiences who interact with the *five-stage model* and who listen to jail calls that abuser tampering and manipulation are more understandable. We hope that with continued efforts to examine the volume of data and case studies, we continue the era of new understandings.

References

Crenshaw, K. 1989. "Demarginalizing the intersection of race and sex: A black feminist critique of antidiscrimination doctrine, feminist theory and antiracist politics." *University of Chicago Legal Forum* 139.

Effiong, J.E., P.N. Ibeagha, and S.K. Iorfa. 2022. "Traumatic bonding in victims of intimate partner violence is intensified via empathy." *Journal of Social Personal Relationships* 39 (12): 3619–3637.

Starks, H., and S.B. Trinidad. 2007. "Choose your method: A comparison of phenomenology, discourse analysis, and grounded theory." *Qualitative Health Research* 17 (10): 1372–1380.

Index

Note: Numbers in *italics* indicate figures on the corresponding page.

For Product Safety Concerns and Information please contact our EU
representative GPSR@taylorandfrancis.com
Taylor & Francis Verlag GmbH, Kaufingerstraße 24, 80331 München, Germany

www.ingramcontent.com/pod-product-compliance
Ingram Content Group UK Ltd.
Pitfield, Milton Keynes, MK11 3LW, UK
UKHW050759180926
475701UK00008B/1132
* 9 7 8 1 0 3 2 3 9 1 6 7 0 *